From Prison to Palace

GLOBAL
PUBLISHING
GROUP

Global Publishing Group

Australia • New Zealand • Singapore • America • London

From Prison

to Palace

A Most Unlikely Coppers Story of Narrowly Escaping Prison to Protecting the Queen

Cat Williams

First Edition 2016

Copyright © 2016 Cat Williams

National Library of Australia
Cataloguing-in-Publication entry:

Creator: Williams, Cat, author.

Title: From Prison To Palace: A Most Unlikely Coppers Story of Narrowly Escaping Prison to Protecting the Queen / Cat Williams.

1st ed.
ISBN: 9781925288179 (paperback)

Self-actualization (Psychology)
Quality of life
Conduct of life

Published by Global Publishing Group
PO Box 517 Mt Evelyn, Victoria 3796 Australia
Email info@GlobalPublishingGroup.com.au

For further information about orders:
Phone: +61 3 9739 4686 or Fax +61 3 8648 6871

I would like to dedicate this book to
our mum, Shelagh Marie Williams.
She never got the chance to watch
us grow up, but I know she would be
very proud of the four of us.

Cat Williams

Acknowledgements

In 2003, I had an idea that I wanted to write a book, but it was just an idea. Twelve years later, I was finally able to turn that dream into a reality. I am immensely grateful to my publisher Darren Stephens and the whole of the Global Publishing team for their support and guidance over the past year.

To my Dad, Bernie, thanks for all the material and for giving me a love of travel, adventure and story-telling. Thanks to Jan, for accepting us as your family even after getting to know us!

Thanks to my brothers Bernie and Kev, and my sister Lisa for putting up with my neurotic childhood and not having me committed.

Thank you to Auntie Trish and Uncle Pat, Auntie May and Uncle Ted, and Auntie Kally and Uncle Eric for all your love and support and for always being a port in a storm.

Thank you to Marcus Weston and all the Chevre at the London Kabbalah Centre. Your spiritual guidance has been priceless.

Thank you John Roberts (701) for having more faith in me than I had in myself and showing me what I was truly capable of.

Thank you to my friends who have always made room for me on my travels. Tracie, my oldest friend, thank you for always helping me see the bigger picture. Jan and Leigh, you've always been family (like it or not). Eleni, thank you for taking me in when I arrived in London and Mags, thank you for your friendship in my time of need, despite having to learn how to walk and talk again. Respect. Lynda, thank you for always having the courage to give it to me straight (I've never liked you). Thank you James and Dean for all the fun London nights. Anna, thank you for being a special part of my journey. And thank you Simona for weathering the tail end of the storm. Last but most definitely not least, Dean, your friendship has been priceless.

I mustn't forget my Australian family who made the move so much easier. Thank you to Lisa and Richard for giving me a safe place to land, thank you Nazie and Bonn for adopting me when I was a waif and stray, thank you Celine, my friend and spiritual adviser, thank you Pete (my little bestie) for always being available for a pint, and Ross and Vanessa for being great mates and roomies.

Finally, thank you Mel, for all your support without which I wouldn't have got past the first chapter. Your faith and encouragement helped me push through all the crippling self-doubt.

Contents

Introduction

BALMORAL CASTLE SCOTLAND

I put one hand over my right eye and squinted till I could just make out the silhouette of the castle through the trees. There was absolutely no ambient light whatsoever. This was the third year that I had worked in Balmoral while the Queen and the Royal family enjoyed their annual Scottish retreat. During the day, it was like working on a Disney set. The sun was shining, deer were prancing across the lawn, salmon were leaping upstream and swallows were singing in the trees. But when the sun began to set behind the hills, the deer fled into the forest and the swallows fell deathly silent, it had a slightly more menacing feel to it. Less Bambi, more Evil Dead.

I had been standing in the Forest of Death and Blood for at least an hour. I was tired, bored to tears and to be perfectly honest, slightly terrified.

Fortunately, I'd been issued with a pair of night vision goggles to enable me to see the full horror of whatever was lurking in the woods. I was a nervous wreck. Every sound, every leaf rustling became a hairy, salivating, gnarly-toothed, dog-zombie coming to drag me into the forest by my entrails.

This is ridiculous!

Why was I was standing in a Scottish wood in the dead of night freezing my arse off, while the Queen and her guests were drinking Chateau Latife by an open fire and all my mates were out clubbing in Soho? If I had followed the original plan, I'd be sunning myself on an Australian beach by now, but life had taken a slight detour.

I took solace from the fact that the Queen could sleep well knowing I was standing on the other side of the castle wall, ready and willing to protect her from whomever would seek to do her harm.

I heard a rustling in the leaves behind me and instinctively jumped onto the nearest tree stump. I looked down through my goggles only to see a bright green field mouse scurrying off into the woods.

For crying out loud!

Whose idea was it to post armed London police officers in Scottish woods at night? We're just not used to wildlife. It's only a matter of time before a poor unsuspecting Corgi gets a magazine emptied into him by a nervous London bobby.

Reload!

Try explaining that to the Queen.

My phone started vibrating in my pocket and I almost un-holstered my Glock.

For god's sake...

It was a text from my mate James.

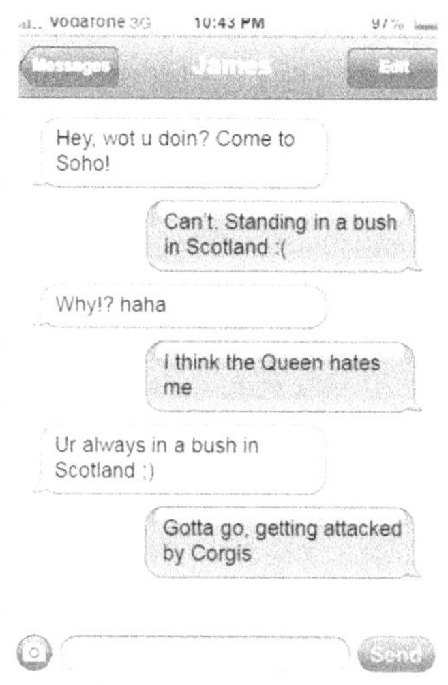

I quickly put my phone away and picked up the goggles. The portico doors opened and nine bright green, furry ankle biters came bounding out of the house.

Here they come. The precocious Royal mutts!

They were on me in an instant, sniffing, pissing and barking at my feet. In the three years I had been working at Buckingham Palace, I had never had a single positive experience with any of the yappy little creatures. I hated them all. They are the most aloof, superior, self-important, crap wherever they like hounds, I have ever come across. I offered one of them a treat one day and it actually turned its over privileged nose up at me and walked away.

Oh, I'm not worthy...

I tried to shake the feeling of insecurity washing over me but I could barely make eye contact with anyone for the rest of the day. Never in my life had a dog made me feel inferior, till then. They're all frequent flyers with jet set attitudes. If you ever bump into them in the First Class lounge at Heathrow, they will look down on you, and I promise, you will feel small.

I turned my torch down at my leg to see one of the Corgis sniffing at my feet.

"Piss off you little mutt!" I shooed him away with the toe of my boot. It immediately started barking and ran off into the forest of Death and Blood.

And don't come back...

"Officer? Where is my officer?"

The Queen was standing about twenty metres away swinging her ten million candle power torch across the lawn.

"I'm over here, your Majesty." I replied and shone my torch at the ground by my feet.

"Ah, there you are," she said and immediately pointed the torch right in my newly adjusted eyes.

JESUS MARY MOTHER OF GOD!

I covered my now watering eyes and started sneezing uncontrollably.

"Are you alright Officer?"

I think my eyes are bleeding!

"Sorry, yes thank you Ma'am. It's just... bright light."

Did you just say, bright light to the Queen of England?

"Yes, well, keep warm officer. The temperature has dropped somewhat. Goodnight."

"Thank you Ma'am. Goodnight," I replied.

How embarrassing...

I watched as the Queen headed back to the house swinging her torch and shouting each of the dog's names in turn. She wasn't above swearing at them if they took their time. I liked that. It made her seem more human, down to earth.

"Come on Willow, move your bloody arse!" The missing Corgi ran out of the forest, stopped at my feet, barked and ran back towards the house.

"Go on you posh little snob!" I said under my breath and flicked my boot at him.

That was their last walk of the night. I heard the portico doors being locked, so I wandered over to the house. I caught sight of my reflection in a window.

You look ridiculous!

I was wearing a Metropolitan Police uniform and I was carrying a Heckler and Koch MP5 carbine semi-automatic rifle, a Glock, 80 rounds of ammunition and a pair of night vision goggles.

Do you think you're in Mission Impossible?

I looked, for all intents and purposes, to be an actual police officer. Truth be known, I never actually wanted to be a police officer and I don't think I've ever been particularly good at it.

You are a complete fraud.

I was due to head back to London the following day but I didn't want to go home. I took up my post near the castle and stared out into the Scottish night sky as the mist rolled in off the hills.

Really? Rolling mist now?

This night shift was panning out like a B-list horror movie. I planted my back firmly against the castle wall and kept my rifle pointed at the scary fog. I'd have felt safer with a crucifix and some holy water.

I am not getting paid enough for this...

I got myself as comfortable as possible under the portico. I now had the rest of the night to think, and think and think.

By morning I had come to the conclusion that 2005 had been a completely shit year. Everyone has them, even the Queen, only when the Queen has a shit year, it's called an Annus Horribilis.

Yes, 2005 had definitely been my Annus Horribilis.

How did everything get in such a mess?

The Long Sulk

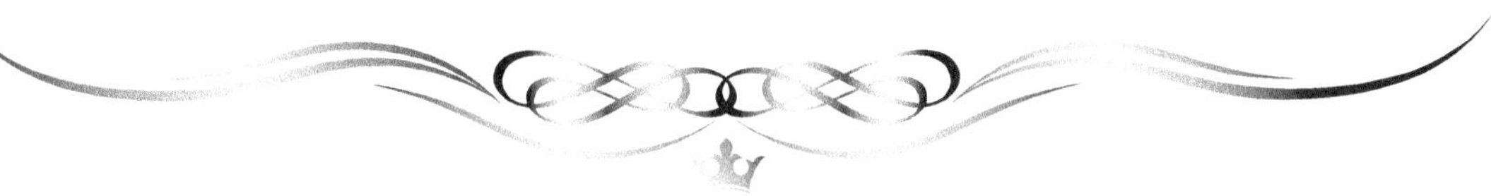

Chapter 1

The Long Sulk

"Adversity has the effect of drawing out strength and qualities of a man that would have lain dormant in its absence."

Herodotus.

Monday the 15th July 1974 started out like any other. I was only five so I didn't have a lot going on in my social calendar, but I would always make time to pick on my little sister Lisa, because I felt it was important for the family dynamic. She was only three but she had mastered the art of the 'back of the arm squeezy pinch' so I had to keep a slight reactionary gap.

That morning, we were having a sisterly bonding session which consisted of me throwing a boomerang hairbrush at Lisa's forehead to see if it came back. It *always* came back.

My older brothers Bernard and Kevin were busy downstairs doing meaningful boy stuff like running face first into walls and giving each other wedgies. Dad was out visiting mum at the Liverpool Royal Infirmary. Sometimes he took us with him, sometimes he went alone. Today was no different.

But, it was…

Chapter 1: The Long Sulk

When dad got back, he came upstairs into our bedroom, sat down on the bed and said, very matter of factly, "Your mum just died."

Then he got up and left the room.

I'm not sure how you're supposed to tell your thirteen, ten, five and three-year-old that their mum just died. Neither did dad. There was no manual for this. Dad was a marine engineer from Liverpool, not a social worker.

This is a very bad day...

So while Nixon was in the White House and Charles Aznavour was singing "She" on the radio, we said goodbye to our mum. She died of breast cancer at the age of thirty-three.

Shelagh Marie Williams

That was the first day of what I like to call The Long Sulk. It was to last another thirty years, give or take a day. It meant I was going to miss out on some of the relevant software conducive to a happy childhood such as self-esteem, self-worth and confidence. To be honest, the whole system was going to need a reboot.

St Peter and Pauls Primary School

Over the next couple of years, I developed an unhealthy obsession with death. I desperately needed answers, and Father Carroll's bog standard, "Your mum is with Jesus now" explanation made absolutely no sense to me. Was she in Jerusalem!?

These were the guys with all the answers. They had a direct line to God. Why wouldn't they tell me where she was? I decided I would have to become a priest. It was the only answer.

Not long after my first holy communion, Father Carroll came to class and asked who wanted to become an altar boy. I put my hand up. One step closer to God. I sat there patiently with my hand in the air and watched as each boy was summoned to the front to be taken into the fold. My name wasn't called. I didn't even make it through the paper sift. Father Carroll flatly rejected my application in front of the whole class on account of my name being Catherine, not Colin. That made me furious.

That is the last time I put my hand up in class!

And it was.

I was hardly in a position to picket the church or go banging on the door of the Equal Opportunities Commission. I had to suck it up. I left the church with a lump in my throat which I quickly coughed away when I saw my nemesis, Ian Walker, standing with his new gang of altar boys. He was leaning against the wall of the church proudly showing off his new boy frock with matching accoutrements. He sneered at me and started whining in a high pitched nasal voice, "I'm Catherine, I want

to be an altar boy, I want my mummy..." and then he and the rest of the gang started laughing and pointing at me.

Little brat...

I'm not exactly sure what happened next. Something snapped inside my tiny little head and I could feel the veins on my forehead throbbing. My heart was beating so fast it felt like it was going to explode and I had just about bitten through my bottom lip by the time I had covered the ten meters to where Ian was standing.

The anger had reached boiling point and was looking for an outlet, a little like a bolt of lightning looking for the quickest way to earth itself. I decided to earth myself against the back of Ian's head, so I swung my arm back as far as I could and let it fly back with laser-like precision.

Ian must have sensed the awesome weaponry that was about to be unleashed on him. He started to turn around and instead of punching him in the back of the head as I intended, all four little knuckles found themselves firmly planted in Ian's right ear with the explosive force of a miniature sledge hammer. Ian let out such a high pitched squeal, it brought Father Carroll out of the church to see which one of the girls had hurt themselves. He looked quite surprised to see Ian holding his ear, sobbing.

By the time Father Carroll caught up with me, I was standing next to the font with my right arm up to my elbow in Holy water, praying for the pain to go away.

Lord have mercy!

He took one look at me, grabbed my collar and frog marched me to the Headmistress's office, leaving a trail of holy water across the playground.

No regrets...

That was the first time I remember losing my temper, but it wouldn't be the last.

Later on that week, clutching my rosary beads, I begrudgingly took my turn in the confessional. Father Carroll prompted me, "Forgive me Father for I have sinned… go on Catherine."

He was expecting me to confess to bursting Ian's ear drum, but I was totally unrepentant. "Where... is... my…MUM?" I refused to leave the box until Father Carroll answered me. He couldn't answer me, so he did the next best thing. He physically ejected me from the confessional in a very unchristian like manner.

I'm telling Jesus about this!

That was the day I officially fell out with God. I no longer wished to be a friend of the Lord. To be truthful, I was hoping for some kind of reaction. Kids need boundaries after all. I didn't want to be struck down by lightning but a crack of thunder would have been nice.

There was nothing. Not a thing. Total indifference.

There is no such thing as God!

Being completely ignored by the Almighty absolutely infuriated me, so I did what any self-destructive seven-year-old would do in those circumstances. I punched my two older brothers in the nuts. That always had the desired outcome.

When I was feeling in a slightly better mood, I would just sit in the dark setting light to Lisa's dolls or dripping candle wax over anything that moved. That always cheered me up, but Lisa was starting to look like a display at Madame Tussaude's.

Brunei, Borneo

Dad did his best to keep us all together over those three years, but it was getting harder to find suitable people to live in while he was away at sea. He started applying for land based jobs. Just before my eighth birthday, dad got us all together and told us he had been offered a job in Brunei, Borneo. He was taking Lisa and me with him, but there were no decent schools for Bernard and Kev, so they had to stay in the UK. I was excited to be going with dad but inconsolable at the thought of being taken away from my brothers. Sadly, the sentiment wasn't returned.

Bernie, Kev and me

I wanted to see where we were going to live, so dad got out a world map and pointed to a green dot just above Indonesia. It was obscured by a thick red line that dad told me was called the equator. I had no idea what that meant until the plane doors opened.

Holy Mary, Mother of God!

It was like breathing molten lava. My eight-year-old lungs had never been subjected to such punishment. My thermostat was set at an average 10 degrees Celsius all year round which appeared to be the optimum temperature for unhindered breathing. What kind of fiery hell had dad brought us to? Brunei had three seasons. There was hot season, even hotter season and hot and wet season.

Most of the ex-pats were enrolled at the International School because it had an English curriculum and a fairly good reputation. School started at 7.30am and finished at about 2.00pm because of Borneo's ridiculous equatorial climate. The building wasn't air conditioned, they just kept all the windows and doors open for ventilation and let us sweat.

I hated everything about Brunei. I hated the blistering heat and constant sunburn. I hated the killer bull ants, deadly millipedes and crab-clawed scorpions that made every barbecue a lottery of pain and terror. I hated having to dodge the nest of tarantulas that had taken up residence in the garage and the Japanese hornets that forced me to throw myself face first into a storm drain. But most of all, I hated that huge Portuguese man o'war that turned a perfectly pleasant day at the beach into a near death experience.

Lisa and I spent most of our childhood being chased by venomous, tropical creatures trying to inflict painful, stingy deaths on us. It was exhausting just trying to stay alive. I desperately wanted to go home, so I concocted a cunning plan to make everyone's life a misery and whinge every single day till dad sent me back to England.

Three years later, my resolve had started to weaken, but I felt confident that I was starting to wear Lisa down. We shared a bedroom so she had no escape from my morbid moods swings. Most nights, I liked to just sit up and stare at her while she was trying to sleep. She didn't like that.

Christmas in Brunei was different. Less snowballs, more third degree

burns. Dad always made a big effort though, we were spoilt rotten. One year we came home from school and Bernie and Kev were there unpacking their bags. Best Christmas present ever. They had to go back after New Year though which of course meant more tearful airport departures. That was the Christmas dad bought Lisa and me a state of the art, Hitachi stereo cassette recorder for us to share. I'd often walk in and find Lisa dancing around to Abba, but all that 'Mamma Mia' crap was far too cheery for me. I wanted to listen to 'Welcome to my Nightmare' by Alice Cooper. Someone broke into the house and pulled all the Abba tapes apart. It was really weird.

That same week, Lisa decided to borrow my bike without permission. Lisa had her own bike so she was obviously trying to prove a point. 'Sibling points' aren't just ordinary points. These are well thought out, meticulously planned, button pushing points. They are designed to infuriate regardless of the consequences.

I ran out the front of the house and grabbed hold of the handlebars as Lisa rode past. I hadn't really thought things through properly though. The bike came crashing down on its side with Lisa still firmly attached. She got up and ran inside the house crying and holding her arm.

"DAD! Catherine's broken my arm!"

"Don't be silly poppet, it's not broken."

Click... went the remote control.

Understandably, dad was in his own little bubble which he only ventured out of to turn the TV channel over or grab a Tiger beer. The next morning Lisa's arm was still extremely swollen and misshapen. We took her to the hospital and the x-ray confirmed that she was suffering from a serious case of sibling rivalry. Her arm was broken in two places.

Sisters...

Step mum

Dad had dated a few ladies over the years and one evening he introduced us to a very glamorous young oriental lady called Ling Ling. She reminded me of the Singapore Airlines trolley dollies. Within minutes, she had sat me on her knee and cut my finger nails. No one had ever done that before. I was completely sold. She had me at ni hao.

Ni hao- hello -[Mandarin]

It wasn't long before Ling moved in and we had to get used to a few cultural differences. I wasn't used to seeing my Sunday roast running around the back garden for starters. Sunday roasts had always come

featherless and vacuum packed from the local supermarket. Ling preferred fresh. She would pop out the back with her meat cleaver, and five minutes later the garden was covered in feathers and there would be a stuffed chicken in the oven. It horrified me. I almost became a vegetarian.

Ling was a fantastic cook. Even if there was nothing in the fridge, she could knock a Chinese meal together with some sardines and an OXO cube. Dad began inviting friends over for dinner parties and we finally got to hear some of his war stories. Dad was quite the story teller. There wasn't a corner of the globe that he hadn't ventured to and brought stories back from. They fascinated me.

I came home from school one day and Ling was preparing a dinner party for dad's work mates. I went to run the bath and there was a shark swimming in it. An actual shark… swimming in the bath.

"DAD! Can I use your shower? There's a shark in the bath!"

"Of course pet."

Click...

After a short engagement, dad and Ling Ling got married. Lisa and I were overjoyed we would be able to call someone mum again. Our overjoyness lasted until Ling Ling reached the end of the church aisle. Lisa and I ran over and said "Congratulations mum!" like a pair of desperate orphans.

Ling Ling gave us what I can only describe as a grima-smile. Half smile, half grimace.

You're not my real mum!

To be fair, taking on a ten-year-old moody step daughter at the age

of twenty-three was no small undertaking. In fact, I'm fairly certain Mother Teresa would have punched me in the throat.

Coincidentally, that same year Lisa and I were put on a plane back to the UK where we were to spend the next five years incarcerated in a boarding school in Cheshire.

Beacon of Light

Waking up in the darkness feeling scared and so alone,
Wandering barefoot from room to room, wondering
where you've gone.
The unbearable truth, it was just a dream,
she's never coming home.
A deafening silence echoes around your cold and empty room.

So sad to see her flame burn out, she was only thirty-three.
Such a beautiful life cut far too short by a tragic irony,
Nursing each of us from her breast, not knowing the
price she'd pay,
The breasts that gave her children life would take her life away.

The safe harbour now behind you, you're heading for
treacherous seas,
Best batten down the hatches, and wait for the storm to ease,
It's true that clear and calm waters never did a skilled
sailor make,
Adversity, my greatest teacher, helped me weather the
storms in my wake.

For the love I'd known those first five years, unconditional,
pure and complete,
I have searched in many foreign lands to be saddened by defeat,
For the Holy Grail I made my quest, was always
within my reach,
It was the love inside that I've always had unconditional,
pure and complete.

My Guiding Star in uncharted seas, you were my
Beacon of Light,
Always shining, ever present throughout the darkest of nights,
You gave me strength to carry on when I felt all hope was gone,
Even though I felt so lost inside, you helped me find
my way home.

Although you left many years ago, your light shines on in me,
The light of a thousand candles burning eternally,
These eyes have no regrets for all the tears they've cried,
For behind these deep cool waters is the flame of hope that
never dies...

That flame will pass from hand to hand to cast light
into the shadows,
To guide those stricken vessels through the dark
and rocky shallows.
To give lost sailors hope and faith to continue with their plight,
Keep pushing through those stormy seas toward that shining
Beacon of Light...

Doddington Hall

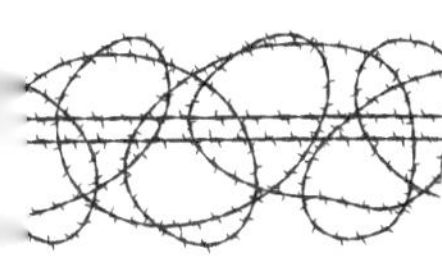

Chapter 2

Doddington Hall

"Noblesse Oblige - Privilege entails responsibility"

- St George's house motto

In fairness, boarding school had always been on the cards. Most of the ex-pats sent their kids to boarding school at age ten or eleven, because the education system in Brunei wasn't up to the same standard as back home. Dad sent off for a dozen prospectus and allowed me to choose which school we went to. I chose Goudhurst College in Cheshire, mainly because it had pictures of smiling school girls riding horses and sailing on the boating lake. I think it's called false advertising. The house, Doddington Hall, was built in 1798 to a Samuel Wyatt design and was the seat of the Broughton Baronets, so it was steeped in history.

I remember the drive to the airport being fairly quiet. "Oh Yeah," (there's a band playing on the radio) by Roxy Music was on and I was finding it difficult to maintain my distant and aloof composure. We'd never travelled without dad before, and being sent off alone to fend for ourselves was playing havoc with my abandonment issues. Dad handed us over to the Singapore Airlines cabin crew and they proceeded to cover us with little red and white stickers symbolizing our induction into the world of jet-setting, 'unaccompanied minors'. We were herded

on and off flights like cattle and rushed through International check-ins like first class passengers. Over the next five years we racked up about 250,000 air miles flying to and from boarding school.

Deep vein thrombosis hadn't been invented back then.

Auntie May and Uncle Ted picked us up from Manchester airport and two days later, still struggling with jetlag, they drove us out into the Cheshire countryside. It was mid-winter and all the hedgerows and fields along the side of the roads were covered in frost and snow. The entrance to the school was through a gated lodge house at the end of a long drive which ran alongside the boating lake. It was just like in the pictures. Horses and donkeys were grazing in the icy paddocks next to the lake. It looked like a scene from a fairy tale. As we pulled up at the front of the house, the place seemed to be in a state of chaos. Suitcases and school chests were being unloaded from cars and parents were shouting their goodbyes to their daughters, who were already half way up the stairs gossiping with their friends. "Yah, bye mummy, ciao."

It was completely alien to us. We weren't posh by any stretch of the imagination.

We'll never fit in…

We were met at the door by one of the girls who had been tasked to meet and greet. "Good morning, I'm Emily. I'll show you the way to the Salon," she said.

We followed close behind until we reached a set of very ornate oak double doors. The Salon was a large circular room with enormous bay windows looking out onto the rear garden and soft tennis courts. Hanging in the centre of the salon was a crystal chandelier that caught

the light from the windows and sent shimmering little rainbows all over the walls.

The chattering of voices became louder as we entered the room and we were taken to a lady who had a very commanding presence about her. She stood very upright with perfect posture and seemed to be as tall as most of the men in the room. She had short grey hair with a slight blue rinse and wore her reading glasses around her neck which she fiddled with constantly. Her rather appropriate country wear consisted of a brown skirt and a tweed jacket and she was surrounded by little pug faced dogs.

Oh my god, it's the Queen.

"Miss Barbara, this is Catherine and Lisa Williams," said Emily.

"Ah yes, thank you Emily," Miss Barbara said. "Well, you have come a long way girls." She then shouted over my head, "Brigitte, come here dear."

I was suddenly joined by Brigitte Morgan, who looked extremely unimpressed to have been assigned to me. She was standing to attention with her shoulders back and chest pushed out and she was wearing a 'Class Captain' badge on her blazer. She reminded me of a Company Sergeant Major with pig tails. She looked me up and down disapprovingly through her spectacles then offered me her limp hand which she suspended in midair.

"Good morning, I'm Bwigitte," she said. I wasn't sure whether she wanted me to shake her hand or kiss it. I shook it and quickly let go.

Bwilliant...

"Catherine, Brigitte will be your house mother. She will show you around the house and answer any questions you may have. Brigitte and her sister Karen also live in Brunei."

The instant dislike was mutual. Lisa was assigned someone in her form to look after her and we were all allowed a cup of tea and a sandwich with Auntie May and Uncle Ted before saying goodbye.

As we left the Upper Hall, Brigitte pointed to a room on the left at the top of the stairs. "That's the weeding woom," she said.

"Weeding woom? What's that?" I asked, totally bewildered.

"It's where you take your books and weed them silly," she said.

Oh of course, reading room, and don't call me silly…

West Wing

Brigitte introduced me to Miss Gleaves (Gleavie), the west wing live-in matron. She was buxom, five-foot-tall, and in some respects looked a little like a smaller version of Miss Barbara without the blue rinse. She had quite a broad northern accent which came out more when she started shouting. Her favourite phrase after "LIIIIIIGHTS OOOOOOOUT!' was "GET BACK IN T' BED YA DIRTY ARABS!"

Political correctness hadn't been invented back then either.

We soon got into the routine of boarding school. The timetable was completely regimented and probably hadn't changed in forty years.

You wake up to a bell. You go to class to a bell. You eat to a bell. Pavlov could have sacked his dogs and given us the job. I'm sure even now, if you rang a bell in any Goudhurst girl's ear, she'd be licking the plate before the dog had even looked up.

Every Friday we had to write a letter home which was vetted by Miss Mason, our form teacher. She corrected my grammar and then I watched in disbelief as she completely rewrote my entire letter.

Dear Dad,

I hate it here, please get me out! If you don't, I'll run away. I think Sister Dargavell is a witch. She used to work in a morgue. She says she preferred working with dead people because they didn't talk back.

Dad, she'd be happier if we were all dead! Last night she shone a lantern next to my face to see if I was breathing. I was too scared to breathe dad.

She's like Florence Nightingale of the dead. She keeps telling us stories about dead people sitting up and opening their eyes. Do they dad? Do dead people sit up and stare at you?

Please let us come home,

Love Catherine

Censored version:

Dear Daddy,

Our first week has been splendid. I have made a lot of friends and they are all terribly gay. We are visiting Crewe tomorrow with Miss Dargavell. She is our new Matron and a jolly good laugh. She tells us the most interesting stories about working in The Alexander Hospital. She checks on us in our beds each night and makes sure we are all safe and sound.

Anyway Daddy, I'll be sure to write you again soon. Don't worry about Lisa and me, we seldom get homesick. We are enjoying our studies and learning a great deal. All the teachers have been wonderful and have commented on how well we have settled in. Much love to Mummy,

With lots of Love,

Catherine x

What Liverpudlian kid that had just crawled out the jungles of Borneo would use the words *splendid, jolly, seldom* and *terribly gay*?

Surely daddy would notice there was something jolly well wrong?

Click...

Maybe not.

I was not impressed with HMP Goudhurst's strict censorship and I had been sentenced to five years without parole. I would have to find another way to communicate with the outside world. I asked Brigitte if we were ever allowed off the school grounds during term time.

"Oh yes, of course. We have three exeats per term," she said.

"Three wha'?" I asked.

"Three exeats silly."

"What exactly is an exeat?"

"It comes from the Latin exire, "to go out." Didn't you learn any Latin at the International school?""

"Er, no, we weren't exactly expecting to be invaded by Rome."

Don't call me silly!

There was no point trying to escape. Where would I go? The location of the school was a deterrent in itself, a bit like Alcatraz. Once you made it off the grounds, there was nowhere to go. We may not have been surrounded by shark infested waters, but the nine-mile hike to the nearest town in a pair of Clarkes school shoes was enough to dampen the spirit of even the most hardened escapee.

I resigned myself to my fate and tried to settle into school life, but it didn't take long before I had stepped out of line. I scratched my initials into a table in Skye Parlour, the third form TV room when I was bored. They called the whole of West Wing into Skye Parlour to ask who'd done it. I had no intention of owning up but I was just so gob-smacked that the genius sleuths of the third form staff room couldn't work out who might have scratched the initials CW.

"Hmmm, let me see," said Miss Mason. "It was done with a serrated edge knife of some sort."

All she was missing was a deer stalker and a pipe.

"Yes, and that looks like an M and a C backwards," added Mrs. Young.

I almost bit through my bottom lip.

Not a single Cluedo player amongst them.

"Actually," I said, "It's a C and a W and I did it with a pair of non-serrated scissors."

They all stopped and looked at me in disbelief.

"Well, I see. So, are you proud of yourself Catherine, owning up like that?" asked Miss Mason.

"Am I proud of what miss? Scratching the table or owning up?"

"Well you don't seem in the least bit remorseful young lady."

I got one week's detention and lost my television rights but somehow it felt as though I was being punished more for owning up than for scratching the table.

Coming of Age

It fell upon the school to teach us about the facts of life, which I found absolutely fascinating, but I didn't think any of it applied to me. In fact, I forbid myself to ever have a period.

You are NEVER having a period!

Periods were for girly girls who wanted to get married and have loads of kids. I certainly wasn't one of them. A sudden onset of luteinising hormone in forth form proved me completely wrong, but at least I was listening in biology.

This cannot be happening...

I was the first girl in my class to start my period which I found mortally embarrassing. My coming of age was made all the more shameful and humiliating when Gleavie introduced me to the appropriately named 'Monthly Book' which we all had to sign each time we had a period.

I don't think so...

It seemed a little too Orwellian to me and I was not about to have Big Brother knowing all my bodily functions. What next? A Daily Bowel Movement register?

The Monthly Book was supposed to ensure none of the girls were 'up the duff'. It was also to keep a track of those girls who disliked swimming lessons so much that they had periods every Monday and Friday. I was never going to sign that book. Each month I walked past without signing, I was filled with guilt. I even started sneaking down the 'out of bounds' stairs just so I wouldn't have to walk past it.

Don't be ridiculous, it's only a book. A book of shame...

When I had officially *missed* two periods, I was introduced to the fine system that was in place for not signing the book. I was fined £0.75 which I refused to pay. My name was published in the Monthly Book fine register which was then placed outside the staff room. It made me

cringe every time I walked past it, but someone had to take a stand. I'm proud to say, I still owe £0.75.

One night Gleavie accused me of being insolent for not signing the book and refusing to pay the fine. I accused her of being a Nazi and said it was like living in a police state. She raised her hand above her head and I honestly thought she was going to hit me.

What a liberty!

I batted her hand away and immediately walked back to my dorm. The next morning, I was sent to Miss Barbara's office to explain how I had come to break one of Gleavie's fingers. I was mortified. I hadn't meant to hurt her. That was my first big misdemeanour.

Strike one!

St Trinian's

Prior to the eighties, Goudhurst had been a very reputable school, but then the school ran into financial difficulties. Miss Barbara began to take on problem girls who had been expelled from other schools, so long as their parents had sufficient funds to pay the fees. There were at least three girls whose local councils were actually paying their school fees. I think the technical term is 'displacement' where you simply move the problem to another area so it becomes someone else's problem. Call me a cynic.

One morning when we were about to start lessons, there was an unmistakable sound of helicopter rotors whipping the air outside the classroom window. Right there, landing on our hockey pitch was 'someone else's problem'. Her name was Georgina. She jumped out of the helicopter and threw her faux fur throw around her neck like some kind of Hollywood movie star and headed toward the house. I could just make out Miss Barbara walking over to greet her. Some girls arrived in Range Rovers, some in Rollers and even the odd Bentley, but never a helicopter. I hated her already.

Later on that day I was introduced to my new cellmate, Georgina, who preferred to be called 'George'. George had been expelled from two other boarding schools so Goudhurst was her last chance. She was basically rebelling against mummy and daddy and had absolutely no respect for rules of any kind. I tried not to like her but in truth I was in awe of her devil-may-care attitude.

We were in the lab one Friday morning when Mrs Thwaites, the mad chemistry teacher, showed us the reaction between water and potassium. Who knew you could set water on fire?

Fantastic!

We were so impressed that George and I decided to do our own little science project on the lake. After church the following Sunday, we broke into the chemistry lab and borrowed a jar of potassium from the chemical cupboard and headed down to the boat house. There was an old wooden rowing boat moored inside. I was only going to pour a few potassium balls into the water next to the boat to see what would happen, but as I opened the jar, some of the oil spilled out. I could feel the jar slipping through my fingers but there was nothing I could do to stop it. The whole jar fell into the water and disappeared under the boat.

Oh dear Lord...

There was a fizzing, popping sound and smoke started coming out of the water next to the boat. We watched in horror as the boat filled with water and slowly disappeared under the surface. I had sunk the HMS Goudhurst and it was now in a watery grave at the bottom of the lake. Perhaps not one of the worst maritime disasters in history but it cost me a trip to Alton Towers theme park with the rest of the school. That hurt. I'd been looking forward to it for weeks.

Strike two!

I watched out of my dormitory window as four coach loads of giggling, singing schoolgirls headed up the driveway out of sight. It was the longest day ever waiting for the coaches to come back. I sat there all day, throwing stones in the lake, listening to Human League's 'Dare' on my Sony Walkman.

I was starting to wonder if honesty was the best policy. I seemed to be spending a lot of my free time in the library having detention. I hated it, because it was always the same punishment. Writing out of the Oxford English Dictionary, word for word. I started off with Aardvark in the third form, by the time I reached fifth form, I had practically re-written the whole OED. Well, I'm exaggerating a little. I'd gotten as far as Pyromania, but I'd also added a few of my own words, which I felt had been carelessly omitted. That got me extra detention too.

pyro|mania

noun (Psychiatry) the uncontrollable impulse and practice of setting things on fire

Coming Out

By the time I reached forth form, I finally found a way to channel my slightly self-destructive tendencies. I was actually good at athletics and horse riding, so I was spending a lot of time at the stables or the oval. The girls in my form used their time at the stables as a chance to meet boys. I had absolutely no interest in boys at all. I was a sulky little tomboy and while all the girls had pictures of Duran Duran or Depeche Mode on their walls, I had a picture of Boy George wearing a fantastic shade of Pacific Prawn lipstick. The only boys I was interested in were trying to look like girls.

I decided to have a chat to Sister Bissett, our full time Matron. Sister Bissett was everything you would expect a Matron to look like if you have ever seen any of the 'Carry on' films. She wore a dark blue nurse's uniform which was immaculately pressed with an old style nurse's hat clipped to her hair. Pinned to the front of her uniform was a nurse's fob watch which she wore like a prized medal.

Sister Bissett could usually be found in 'stickies' the nurse's room, dispensing paracetamol and eucalyptus cotton balls. She walked so fast it sounded as though she was tap dancing. If you wanted to speak to her outside 'stickies' hours, you had to keep up. I caught up with her just as she was opening the door.

"Good morning Catherine, what can I do for you this fine morning?" she said with a very strong Scottish Highland accent.

"Sister, I think I'm gay."

Sister Bissett continued sifting through her medicine drawer without turning around.

"That's nice dear."

When the penny finally dropped, she gave me two paracetamol, shoved a thermometer in my mouth and quarantined me in sickbay until the school could get an appointment with the local psychiatrist. Dr. Handley had absolutely no idea what to do with me, so we just sat there staring at each other awkwardly for an hour. Then she sent the school a £100 bill which Miss Barbara charged to my school fees under the heading 'miscellaneous expenses.'

I was allowed back into the school environment under strict supervision until the psych report came back. Rebecca, one of the prefects, was assigned to surveil me around the school grounds. She wasn't very good at it. Every time I turned around she tried to hide behind the nearest post, pillar or tree, but her girth gave her away. I wasn't going to make it easy for her, so I decided to go for a long walk to the castle which was out of bounds. I climbed through the castle railings and started up the stairs to the second floor. I was going to give Rebecca a cheeky wave from the window, but as I reached the top stair, my feet started slipping and sliding on something dark and damp on the landing.

What the...

I poked my head slowly around the corner. There were feathers blowing around from ceiling to floor. As my eyes adjusted to the darkness, I could just make out large clumps of wet, black feathers all over the floor. There were at least ten dead crows lying in the middle of the room in a makeshift circle.

Unusual...

It was mid-January, so my first thought was that maybe they had frozen to death. That was until I noticed that all of their heads had been arranged in a neat little pile in the corner of the room.

For the love of Beelzebub!

One thing that scared me more than bible bashers was devil worshippers. In my haste to leave the castle with all of my limbs intact, I made a slight error in judgement as I pole vaulted the railings. My kilt got caught and I found myself impaled upside down.

Please god, don't let Damien find me here like this…

I started screaming for help. No-one came. I desperately struggled with the buttons on my kilt until I fell to the ground in a heap in just my underwear. I unhooked my kilt from the railings and started running like Roger Bannister. I didn't stop running and I didn't look back until I reached the house.

When I opened the front door, sweating and gasping for breath, I was surprised to see Sister Bissett and Rebecca both standing there.

"Ok Catherine, upstairs to sick bay with you," Sister Bissett said.

She grabbed one arm, Rebecca grabbed the other and they frog marched me through the lower hall and up three flights of stairs, in just my school underwear.

Oh the indignity…

The following day Miss Barbara called my dad to inform him that I was involved in witchcraft.

"Well, Mr. Williams, Catherine chopped the heads off a dozen crows and was seen to dance around half naked at the castle, which as you know, is out of bounds."

My dad still goes on about that now, "Catherine, what were you thinking killing all those crows?"

"I nev…"

Click…

The Final Straw

I was released from solitary confinement a few days later. That evening, Miss Barbara was holding her once yearly cheese and wine 'do' for all the gentry, so we were all banished to Top Floor, not to be seen or heard.

The following morning, on our way down to breakfast, George and I took a peek into the Upper Hall out of curiosity. It was immaculate, apart from the bar at the far end. We didn't need to say a word. We both started grabbing bottles of Cherry B, Baby Sham and Pale Ale as if we were on Supermarket Sweep. We hid most of it in our form room and then sneaked into breakfast thinking our absence hadn't been noted.

About 10.00am, I was in my computer lesson when one of the prefects knocked on the door. "Miss Barbara wants the whole school to assemble in the Broughton Room straight away," she said.

My heart skipped a beat. The last time Miss Barbara had cause to summons the whole school was after a school trip to the opera in

London. She had been informed that Her Majesty's Theatre was most definitely not amused that we had liberated them of almost 140 pairs of opera glasses.

"I will not rest until every single pair of glasses are recovered and returned to Her Majesty's Theatre!"

We all willingly emptied our knicker draws and handed the glasses back in. This was different though. This was just me and George, no-one else. As I headed out into the hallway I caught George's eye. She gave me a knowing look, smiled and shrugged her shoulders. That was typical of George. Nothing seemed to phase her. Not even the possibility of being expelled a third time. I was sure that she would walk to the hangman's noose with the same laissez faire attitude. A quiet, resolved dignity.

We filed into the Broughton room and were surprised to see Miss Barbara already standing on the dais. She was watching every single girl as they came in and she looked furious. All the members of staff were standing at the back of the room. No-one spoke. The atmosphere hadn't been this tense since someone set light to the stable block. Fortunately, I had an alibi for that one. We all stood in front of our seats until every girl was present. When each form teacher nodded that all her girls were there, Miss Barbara gave us permission to sit.

"This is a very dark day for the school," she started off. "A very dark day indeed."

I found myself becoming more religious with her every word.

Dear God...

"The school's reputation has been tarnished by the actions of one or two girls," she continued. As she looked around the room, she fixed her eyes firmly on George and me.

Please Jesus...

"The Black Bull have contacted the police regarding the theft of alcohol from the Upper Hall overnight. I want every single bottle back by 11.00am. That is all." She fixed George and me with another steely stare as she left the dais.

George and I handed ourselves in and were duly interrogated by Cheshire Police who tore a strip off the pair of us. Shortly after, all the girls were assembled again and Miss Barbara wasted no time in verbally destroying us both in front of the whole school. I stood belligerently, arms crossed staring straight ahead. I had completely zoned myself out for the public humiliation. She completely annihilated us. I had forgotten how many words started with dis.

"Disrepute, disgraceful, dishonourable, dishonest, disgusted, disappointed, disbelief."

When Miss Barbara finished she just stepped off the dais and left the room.

Strike three! And you're out!

Miss Barbara suspended both of us the next morning. One week later, my psychiatrist report came back. Dr. Handley recommended that I be placed in either a secure juvenile unit or a coeducational school, where I could mix with boys, thereby curing me of my unnatural attraction to other girls.

A Master's degree in psychology, and all she could come up with was to place me in a mixed school full of post pubescent, hairy-lipped, teenage boys that spent most of the time either scratching their bollocks or talking about them.

Yep, that'll fix me...

I immediately opted for electric shock therapy instead but that apparently went out in the sixties. Despite me offering to plug myself into the mains, it fell on deaf ears.

My last report card read something like:

Catherine is still very much involved in County Athletics and equestrian sports. She has also taken up a wee bit of lesbianism in her free time and is an active member of the local coven.

You couldn't make it up.

So, on the 1st February 1984, I was expelled for an accumulation of things, including the false allegation of witchcraft.

Unbelievable.

I had been expelled from a boarding school that was a haven for all the other expellees in the country. How bad did that make me?

You're going to hell...

I came to the conclusion that life was pretty shit.

"I don't mean to sound bitter, cold, or cruel, but I am,
so that's how it comes out."

Bill Hicks

Down The Rabbit Hole

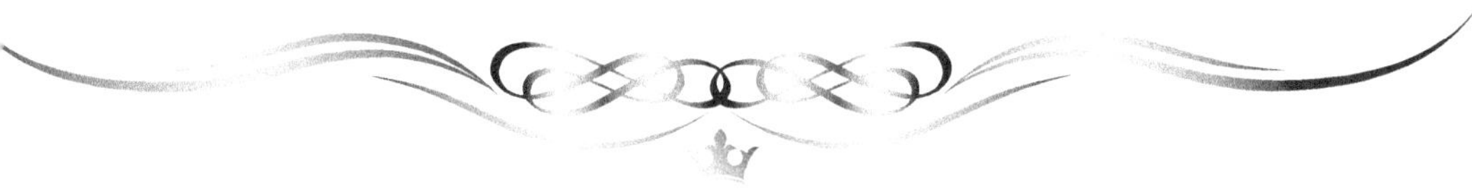

Chapter 3

Down The Rabbit Hole

"If you don't know where you're going, any road will take you there."

Cheshire Cat

Dad was surprisingly understanding when he came to pick me up from school. He knew I was heart-broken. Goudhurst was home. It's where all my friends were, where Lisa was. He only had a couple of weeks to find me a decent school, so he took me to Brereton Hall in Sandbach where I had an interview with the head mistress. I remember her having quite a strong German accent. She asked me what my favourite subject was.

"Biology miss," I answered.

"Oh, we don't study sciences here at Brereton Hall. We find our girls don't need them."

Oh my god, I'm in Stepford.

The school was churning out professional wives whose only desire in life was to marry a banker with a double barrelled name, live in Chelsea and drive Ollie and Trixie to school in a Range Rover.

I'm in hell…

I looked over at dad and begged him with my eyes not to send me there. Thankfully, the Headmistress knew Miss Barbara, so it didn't take long for her to find out that I was a Satan-worshipping deviant.

My application was rejected on the grounds that the school felt that I would be a negative influence on the younger girls. They were obviously concerned I may try to introduce science as a novel concept.

For the love of Marie Curie!

The Truant

I had the same result at Birkenhead High, which was a reputable girls boarding school closer to home. Dad tried his best but my reputation preceded me. We had run out of time and dad had to jump on another plane. My eldest brother Bernie had followed in my dad's footsteps and he was probably on an oil tanker somewhere in the South China Sea, so I moved in with my older brother Kevin who immediately hid all the matches and started wearing a box again. I was enrolled at St Mary's Catholic Comprehensive.

Oh joy...

The hardest part was getting myself out of bed and to school. There were no bells here, no noise from three baths running and ten hairdryers all going at the same time. No laughter or the sound of bare feet running up and down marble corridors. No matron shouting at you to "Move your bloomin' arse!" It was too quiet. I was even missing Lisa. This was the first time we'd ever been apart. I sat in the kitchen alone eating my breakfast looking down at the emblem on my blazer. It read 'Dominus Regat' and underneath 'Christ Within us All' which was the school motto. I still wasn't speaking to Jesus so I was less than impressed that he was staring at me from my blazer.

I thought back to one particular R.E. lesson at Goudhurst. I was staring out of the window as usual, when The Lord tried to get my attention. Mrs Klafkowska threw a leather bound bible at the back of my head, King James version. That just strengthened my resolve to keep God at arm's length.

St Mary's had Holy Godliness lessons three times a week and as I was still harbouring a grudge and possibly a slight concussion from the bible incident, I felt safer not going into school on days where there were bibles on every table. I had one of the highest absentee rates the school had ever seen.

The pattern of truancy went on for months until one day, I decided to run away to my Auntie Trish and Uncle Pat's house. It had always been like a second home to us. While I was there, I had a visit from a social worker called Liz. She explained that my truanting had become so serious that the Chief Education welfare officer was now involved. That meant I could be placed in care, or worse, locked up in a secure unit for problem kids.

Dear God, no...

That scared me. Liz became like a best friend and in all honesty, I would not have gotten through that last year of school had it not been for her. I confided in her a lot.

One Wednesday evening, she took me to a gay youth group in Liverpool called the Link. I'd never met any other gay people before. It felt a bit strange because the only thing we really had in common was that we were all gay. We were a bunch of misfits, most of whose families had disowned them. My dad hadn't disowned me thankfully, but then he was on the other side of the world. Liz had to keep the headmaster informed

of my progress and in one meeting she mentioned she'd taken me to a gay youth group.

"The gay youth what!?" asked Mr Humphries. The look on his face was priceless. He was the headmaster of one of the largest Catholic Comprehensive in the country, responsible for the salvation of 3000 souls.

"Gay...Youth...Group!?" he said. He looked at me as though he'd just scraped me off the bottom of his shoe.

"I've never heard such nonsense!" he said. "Well she'll have to stop going there straight away. What will her father think?"

"Actually, my dad knows I'm gay," I said.

The look he flashed my way actually made me feel disgusted at myself and I couldn't help looking down at my lap.

The shame...

"Utter nonsense. I'll hear no more about it. And if anyone else in the school finds out you have these... tendencies, you will be expelled forthwith. That goes for your sister too. I believe she is due to start next term?"

With that he showed us out of the office and slammed the door.

Because that's what Jesus would have done...

I headed back to my R.E. lesson under a large cloud. While the teacher was preaching away, I started doodling on my hand. It was a fairly innocuous drawing, just a cross on my palm, but by the end of the lesson,

I'd put little legs on it. I was trying to draw an Isle of Mann flag, but that only has three legs and mine had four so that made it a Swastika.

The R.E. teacher saw it and I was back in front of Mr Humphries. He couldn't even make eye contact with me now.

Well, aren't I a dirty little secret...

Well that's just typical, not only is she an evil lesbian, she's also a closet Nazi! What had he done to deserve this? Somewhere in the corners of his mind, I was goose stepping around the corridors of his perfect catholic school in an S.S. uniform preying on the younger girls. He was looking at me like I was some sort of cancer that had to be extricated from his holier than thou house of God. I received my final warning. It was my last chance.

I give up...

I didn't want to play his game anymore. I couldn't walk around school pretending I was someone I wasn't. I became the invisible kid that no-one knew. I was just a whisper at assembly. I woke up one day and the uniform went back under the bed and I was off on my bike before Kev got up.

Problem Child

I was taking a stroll through Liverpool city centre one Sunday morning at 4.00am, as you do, when a police car pulled up alongside me. "What are you doing out this late love?" the copper asked as he wound the car window down.

"I'm off to church, what does it look like!?" I growled at him without breaking my stride.

Wrong answer...

The car jerked to a halt and I was thrown into the back seat of the police car and taken to the local police station while they confirmed my address and spoke to Kev. They were kind enough to give me a lift home but Kev was none too pleased answering the door to the 'bizzies' at 5.00am.

When the police report of my 'nightly wanderings' hit the Chief Education Welfare officer's desk, he organised for a child psychologist assessment to be carried out. It was an order.

The psychologist was straight out of university and my finger was hovering firmly over the self-destruct button.

"So why are you here Catherine?" she asked.

"Because I've been in a bad mood for ten years."

"Ok, well, have you ever thought of harming yourself?" she asked nervously.

"Yes of course, hasn't everyone?" I said.

"Erm no, actually, what have you thought about?"

"I've just always wondered what it would feel like to be nailed to a cross." I said. "Pretty painful I reckon."

"Right, ok," she said adjusting her glasses. "Have you ever thought of harming anyone else?"

"Yes, all the time."

"Who?" She looked up at me almost surprised.

I started counting on my fingers, "My old matron, she made my life miserable. My old Headmistress, my R.E. teacher, Father Carroll, Dr Handley the psychiatrist."

Have I missed anyone?

Then she took out the cards with the asymmetrical ink patterns on them otherwise known as the Rorschach test.

Here we go again...

"OK, tell me what you see. Just say the first thing that comes into your head," she said as she turned the first card over.

"The devil killing a kitten."

"Ok, and this one?" she said turning over the next card. I couldn't believe she was taking me seriously.

"Blood. Lots of blood," I said

"How about this one?" she said.

"Oh, that's definitely an axe. That explains the blood don't you think?"

She threw a couple more at me but I was getting bored and firing off answers without even looking at the cards. To be perfectly honest, they all looked like butterflies to me, but I wasn't going to tell her that.

One week later, I received a personal invitation to see Mr. Ward, the Chief Education welfare officer. I had failed my psychological assessment. I walked into the office with Liz and was surprised to see the psychologist and Mr. Humphries already sitting in the office.

"Good morning Catherine, I'm Mr. Ward the Chief Education welfare officer," he said. He had a large file in front of him with my name on the top under the heading 'Relevant Infant'.

Relevant Infant? I'm fifteen for Christ's sake.

"Good morning sir," I replied and put my head down and tried to hide behind my fringe.

"Well Catherine, this is your last chance. The school has bent over backwards to accommodate you. Do you want to be put in a children's home?" he asked.

God, no!

I shrugged my shoulders and looked at Liz for some reassurance.

"In the past nine months, you have attended school on average, two days a week," he said. "This is your last year. What were you hoping to do when you leave school?"

I've always wanted to be a marine biologist.

"I don't know sir. I haven't given it a lot of thought."

"You seem to me to be an intelligent and very capable young girl, but if you carry on like this we will have no option but to place you as a ward of court. You will have to live in one of our children's homes."

I was starting to feel like orphan Annie. I resisted the urge to break into song.

The Joyrider

After my little pep talk and mainly thanks to Liz's support, I managed to scrape through a few exams. They weren't enough to get me in to the army though which was basically the only plan I had to keep me out of prison. I needed at least two more O' levels, so I enrolled at the local college. A few months later, clutching my exam results, I headed off to the careers office in the hope that the army would adopt me. The careers lady was sitting behind reinforced glass which I thought was odd. I remember her being quite sour faced with badly applied blue eye shadow. Her hair was tied back so tight she looked like she'd had a face lift.

"So, Catherine, what do you want to do?" she asked.

When I told her I wanted to join the army, she actually laughed at me.

"Not with these qualifications you won't. I can offer you a job stacking shelves if you like."

I was beginning to understand why she was sitting behind bullet proof glass. At that time, I had no effective coping mechanism for dealing with rejection. I sat there for a few minutes while my blood came to the boil and my head went the colour of beetroot. I came to the conclusion that there were three ways in which I could deal with this situation.

a)   Take the job stacking shelves.

b)   Go back to college and get the relevant qualifications.

c)   Head to the nearest construction site, steal a 4 tonne fork lift truck, take it on a joyride, then plough it into the Mersey River and cause £30,000 worth of damage.

As I was being thrown head first into the back of the police van, I was wishing I'd gone with option b.

The coppers took me straight to Arrowe Park Hospital to have my head examined. Despite all the blood I only had superficial cuts to the back of my head where a few pieces of glass had embedded themselves. The doctor was treating me like a wayward criminal youth. He roughly slapped some iodine on the cuts and said, "She'll live. You can lock her up now!"

I told him I didn't appreciate his bedside manner. He told me he didn't appreciate pissed up teenage joy riders taking up space in his emergency department.

Whatever...

"Well, someone was looking over you tonight," one of the coppers said, when we were on our way back to the police station. "If the tide had been in, you'd be at the bottom of the Irish Sea by now."

Lucky me...

They explained my arrest to the custody sergeant, who was about 45 years old with greying hair, beard and moustache. He had possibly eaten one too many pies because the buttons on his shirt were screaming under the tension and I could see little belly hairs poking out between them.

"You understand you've been arrested for theft and criminal damage? Do you have anything to say for yourself young lady?" he said.

"Yes actually, I do..."

Don't say it...

"I had no intention of permanently depriving them of their truck. What do you think I was going to do with it? Park it in me dad's garage?"

How clever was I blind siding them with my legal knowledge?

"Oooh, we've got ourselves a back street lawyer guys," said the Sergeant. "Don't bother representing yourself, princess. Best your daddy hires you a real lawyer. You just wrote off a thirty grand truck whether you had the intention of permanently depriving them of it, or not!"

The cell door slamming shut behind me sobered me up pretty quickly.

Shit, I'm going to prison.

About an hour later they came and took me to an interview room, where I was officially cautioned on tape and given a chance to explain myself. It turns out that a cocktail of rejection and humiliation, coupled with

copious amounts of alcohol, is no defence for wanton and deliberate destruction of property. I was charged with theft and criminal damage to the value of £30,000, which included the thirty metres of council railing that ended up in the river.

After having my mugshot taken, they took me to the fingerprint room. I completely disowned my right hand in disgust as they rolled each ink covered finger on the paper. I looked like I was having a manicure. When the process was over, I asked the Sergeant if he could find time in between donuts to find me a feedback sheet so I could inform my local MP about my less than average experience with Merseyside Police.

"Princess," he said, as he leant over the table, "You may think you're funny, but this is my custody and if I decide that you're still intoxicated, you'll be here until I knock off in the morning. Do you understand?"

"Aye, aye Captain! Captain Birdseye!" I saluted.

Shut up!

"Do you want to be here all night?" he asked

God no!

"Not bothered really," I said "Beats waiting till 7.00 for the bus."

"Sign here," he said and threw the pen on the table. "Get her out of here," he told the young coppers.

I signed for my bail and the coppers were good enough to drop me off at home, but I was still full of angst.

"So, did you never think of getting proper jobs you two? No offence but I reckon I could do a better job. My sociology teacher said they did a study on police officers, and most of them suffer with low self-esteem. Were you bullied at school? Did your mum lock you in a cupboard?"

I've no idea why they didn't just kick me out on the side of the road. I was covered in blood and diesel and had a copper on each shoulder when Kev answered the door. He didn't even bat an eye lid. He just turned around and headed back upstairs to bed. Fair enough, this wasn't the first time I'd been brought home by the rozzers, but I thought Kev's laissez faire attitude sent out the wrong signal to the two bobbies that dropped me off. They looked at each other, smirked and walked back to their car.

"Good luck with your careers guys."

Fascists…

I skulked off upstairs and fell into bed. It felt like I'd only just fallen asleep when my bedroom door was flung open and I could hear Madonna's 'Like a Virgin' playing full blast in the background. As my eyes came into focus, I could just make out Lisa's silhouette in the doorway. Her back combed hair practically took up the entire door frame and the smell of hairspray and Georgio perfume was making my eyes water. She was grinning from ear to ear with a copy of the Liverpool Echo in her hand.

"Oooooh, you are in so much shit!" she laughed and threw the paper on my bed and walked out. I looked at the headline, it read:

'Girl cheats death in Mersey plunge!'

Oh My God!

The picture of the upturned forklift took up the whole front page. It looked pretty impressive if I say so myself. I jumped out of bed and nearly fell over. My head was splitting and I was still wearing the clothes I'd had on the night before.

I need a lawyer.

The Martyr

When I got off the train all the billboards were running the headline. One of the Echo sellers was shouting, "Get your Echooo. Girl cheats death in Mersey plunge! Get your Echooo!" Nice touch, a reminder on every corner of the crap I was in.

When I walked into the solicitor's office, she had the Liverpool Echo on her desk. "Was that you?" she asked, as she pointed at the headlines and burst out laughing. Once she composed herself, she added, "You could be looking at two months custodial, but we'll see what we can do."

I'm actually going to prison…

I wasn't expecting that to be honest. I still felt like a kid, but I was eighteen and in the eyes of the law, no matter how angry you may be, taking something that doesn't belong to you and totally destroying it, is frowned upon. I was going to be stuck on the naughty step for a long time.

I was still enrolled at college but when they found out I was on bail for theft and criminal damage, they decided that studying criminal law at their college was a conflict of interest. They kicked me out.

So much for the Presumption of Innocence.

Months went by as I waited for each court date only to have them adjourned on the day. The longer I waited, the more resigned I became. Maybe going to prison wasn't the worst thing that could happen to me. I'd watched the entire series of Prisoner: Cell Block H. It didn't look that bad. I was confident I would come out of prison quite well read and with a humility born of having one's liberty curtailed at the prime of my life. I was going to be a changed person. This would probably be the most character building experience I would ever go through and I was ready to embrace it.

I'll be like William Tyndale or Nelson Mandela.

While all this martyrdom was going on, my dad decided to hire a Barrister. Queen's Counsel, no less. On the third and final court date, I stood in the dock gripping the rail with my toothbrush in my back pocket.

"Catherine Williams, you are charged with theft and causing £30,000 worth of criminal damage. How do you plead?"

I took a deep breath, looked the Magistrate in the eye and said, "Guilty, sir."

"Case dismissed," he said and he struck his little gavel on the bench.

Excuse me?

"Case dismissed?" I looked over at my Barrister in disgust who was shuffling up his court papers with a smile on his face. He leaned over to shake my dad's hand and then headed for the court room door. I was still gripping the rail when the court clerk said, "You're free to go now Miss Williams."

What a miscarriage of Justice!

My barrister had moved for a dismissal on the grounds that the police had not come forward with the prosecution papers in a timely manner. The Magistrate agreed. It seemed that the only person who found the whole things disagreeable was me. I had not planned on walking out a free woman that day.

What was I going to do now? When you've been institutionalised, the thought of being somewhere with boundaries and rules, is strangely comforting. Army, prison, it was all the same to me.

I begrudgingly had to accept my freedom and appreciate that I'd been given a second chance. It was time to climb out the hole I'd made for myself and do something with my life!

Chapter 4

Brick by Brick

Chapter 4

Brick by Brick

"The brick walls are not there to keep us out. The brick walls are there to give us a chance to show how badly we want something. They're there to stop the other people."

Randy Pausch

The Medical Corps

I had just dodged a bullet at court, but I had no clue what I was going to do now. I had been kicked out of college and the careers advisor had assured me the army would never take me. It all seemed pretty hopeless.

I knew someone that had joined the Territorial Army and used that as a spring board into the regular army. The good thing about being full time in the T.A. was that you only had to sign on for short service engagements of one year at a time instead of committing to three. It sounded perfect. I wanted to be a Medic. I wanted to run out onto the battle field with a stretcher and patch people up. Preferably small people who weighed less than ten stone.

I applied to join the Royal Army Medical Corps and was invited along for a weekend of voluntary torture. As I opened the door to the drill hall, I felt like I had walked onto the set of 'Mash.' Large green tents with red crosses on the top were being set up and privates were running all over with empty stretchers.

I asked one of the Corporals where I needed to go.

"Over there," he said and pointed to a blond haired Lance Corporal who was flirting with 'Hot lips Houlihan'.

"Sorry," I interrupted, "I'm here for the training."

"Name?" he asked.

"Williams, sir."

"Get on the back of the truck" he said and pointed to a 4 tonne army wagon with a few nervous faces already on board. There were a few girls on the truck, but they were more the long haired, full of makeup kind of girls. I didn't really have anything in common with them.

Five o'clock the next morning the Corporals were banging on the billet doors shouting at us all to get out on the parade square in our P.T. kit. They took us for a three mile run which nearly killed me. I was completely unprepared. I hadn't done anything physical since I left Goudhurst. The weekend basically consisted of doing press ups in the mud till all the slackers caught up and being dragged around on the end of a stretcher full of wet sand bags. Not as romantic as I'd imagined. In between press ups and stretcher runs, most of the girls spent their time flirting with the Corporals. I estimated that I had done over 400 press ups over the two days, a countless number of squats and absolutely no flirting. At the end of the weekend we were stood to attention on the parade square and the names of those that had passed were read out. My name didn't come up.

"For those of you whose names weren't called out, sorry, you didn't meet the grade."

FAIL

I was absolutely devastated. The careers woman was right. I was a failure. I was physically and emotionally broken. When I got home, I just lay on the couch and didn't move for two days. I couldn't. I didn't have the strength in my arms to push myself off the couch.

Two weeks later, an application form arrived from the Royal Engineers. I discounted it straight away.

I'm not good enough...

Anyway, I couldn't flirt to save my life. My confidence was completely shot. I wasn't sure my self-esteem could take another battering of complete failure and utter rejection. I wrote out a list of pros and cons. There were so many pros and only one con. The con was 'I might fail.'

Why was I so scared of failing? If I failed, then I wasn't good enough. Failure equalled rejection. I was reading something by Tony Robbins at the time and it explained that we all share the same primal fears. In the past when we lived in tribes, we needed to be accepted by the tribe in order to survive. Being banished literally meant the death of us. We couldn't survive on our own. We no longer live in tribes but that fear of being rejected is still in our DNA. It is a survival instinct.

"Our doubts are traitors losing us the good we oft might win by fearing to attempt."

William Shakespeare

If that was the only thing stopping me, I asked myself, "What is the worst that could happen?" I'd failed before, it hadn't kill me. I may end up coming home with my tail between my legs again, but I'll survive. I sent the application off and received an invite for another weekend away. I had six weeks to prepare.

The three-mile basic fitness test (BFT) had been a real struggle and I hadn't done a push-up for years. I needed help. I went down to my local gym and spoke to one of the personal trainers. He put a programme together for me which I followed to the letter. At the end of the six weeks I felt fitter but I still hadn't managed to complete the three mile run in the required time. I was going to have to rely on sheer grit to get me through.

The Royal Engineers

There was a different atmosphere as I walked in to this drill hall. Young guys were running around the hall in their pressed uniforms and the whole place smelled of starch and boot polish. Corporals were barking out orders. "Get that webbing over here guys, hurry up now. Get moving! Gerrit on the back of the lorry." The whole set up seemed more professional than the Medics. More disciplined.

Before I had even walked two paces into the hall I noticed a very lanky perhaps 6'5" tall Sergeant walking towards me. He was mid-thirties with quite chiselled features and his beret was perfectly shaped. You could cut yourself on the creases on his shirt sleeves and he looked every bit how I imagined a professional soldier should look.

He held his hand out to me. "Sergeant Roberts. You must be Williams?" he asked.

"Yes sir. How did you know that?" I asked.

He laughed and replied, "You're the only female we've got on the weekend, and don't call me sir, I work for a living."

"Sorry Sergeant. Well, thank you for noticing I was female," I said and laughed. He put me at ease straight away.

"Do you have any questions or are you unsure of anything?" he asked.

"I'm a bit nervous about the three mile run. I have been training but I'm not sure I'll do it in the time," I said.

"Yeah you will, we'll get you through it," he said and I believed him. There was something about him that made me want to follow him like the Pied Piper.

Once everyone had arrived Sergeant Roberts paraded us and went through what the weekend would consist of. The basic fitness test, three mile run, stretcher runs on the beach, basic drill and weapons familiarisation. I just needed to get through the run and I knew the rest would be plain sailing. They loaded up the back of the wagon with jerry cans full of water and told us to get on board. So far I hadn't seen a single girl. I preferred it to be honest. I couldn't compete with the flirting going on in the Medics, I would never have fit in. I felt like I was on a more even footing with the Engineers.

The run was a three-mile stretch along New Brighton promenade with the starting point at the swimming baths. All twenty-five of us jumped off the wagons and started doing stretches against the lamp posts and railings. It was an unusually warm Saturday in May and the promenade was full of people walking their dogs and eating ice cream. We were obviously a novelty for everyone as they stared at us all getting off the trucks. I wasn't sure what was making me more nervous, the physical exertion or the possibility of failing.

You can't fail again!

Sergeant Roberts took me aside and said, "Nothing to worry about Willow. Just take a few deep breaths and put one foot in front of the other."

'Willow', the first nickname I'd been given that didn't involve some reference to prison or jail bait. How could I possibly let him down now? We all lined up wearing our orange numbered bibs. Sergeant Roberts set his timer, shouted "Go!" and all twenty-five of us were off running in the heat. By the time we had gotten to the first bend I was already sweating and in need of water. Most of the other runners were way ahead. Sergeant Roberts was off in the distance shouting at some of the other recruits. He made it look so easy running in all of his kit, boots and all. Then he ran to the back of the line where all the slackers were. "Come on Willow, gerrup there! Two more miles and you're signing on the dotted line," he shouted.

There were two guys behind me which gave me some encouragement. Sergeant Roberts was shouting, "Come on lads, do you want a girl to beat you or what?"

I'm not sure who he was trying to motivate, me or them but I suddenly found my second wind from somewhere. The lads couldn't catch me. I was onto the final mile when my legs began to feel like jelly and my lungs started burning. I wiped the sweat out of my eyes and when I looked up, I was right on the spot where the forklift truck had gone over the railings. The whole experience came flooding back. All the feelings from getting chucked out of school, of being a failure, of being told I was unemployable.

Bunch of bastards!

I got so angry that the adrenaline started pumping. I could see the finish line in the distance. It looked so far away. I kept running as though my life depended on it. Sergeant Roberts came back when I was about 200 metres from the finish line. "Move your arse Willow. You've got less than a minute. Move it!"

Hearing those words, I suddenly found a strength I never knew I had. A sheer grit and determination despite my lungs being on fire, I ran as fast as my jelly legs would carry me. I knew I could do it. It was right there within my grasp. The finish line got closer and closer and I could see Corporal Smith smiling with the timer in his hand. My lungs were screaming for air and the sweat was stinging my eyes. Three miles, I'd made it, I was over the line. Corporal Smith clicked the timer and shouted, "FAIL!"

God, not again…

I couldn't believe it. I had run till I had nothing left to give. If that wasn't enough, then I wasn't cut out for the army full stop. I collapsed in a heap on the floor with my head through the railings in case I had to throw up. "Get on your feet Willow. Hands on your head and take a few deep breaths," shouted Sergeant Roberts.

One of the unit medics came over and poured some water over my head and handed me a bottle to drink. I hadn't been this looked after by the Medical Corps.

"How did she do?" Sergeant Roberts asked.
"Fail," Corporal Smith said.
"What was her time?"
"27 minutes 45 seconds," replied Corporal Smith.
Sergeant Roberts just laughed and said, "The girls get an extra minute divvy, she's passed."

Those words were like heaven to my ears. "Well done Willow, I knew you could do it," he said. I couldn't stop smiling all the way back to the drill hall. There were two guys who had failed and they looked as miserable as I had a few weeks earlier. In some ways I thought it felt better having not gotten through the first time. It felt like I had really achieved something because I'd had to work harder for it.

On the Sunday afternoon I had an interview with Captain Wright, the staff administration officer. He looked vaguely familiar but I couldn't place him. The first question he asked me was, "Have you ever taken a vehicle for a joyride?" What kind of random interview question was that? After a short reflective pause, I said the first thing that came into my mind, "Sir, I haven't got a driving licence. I can't drive." He smiled at me and then I remembered where I knew him from. He was the Magistrate that had dismissed the court case. He had known who I was the minute I walked in the room.

"Ok, that's fine, just one more question. Do you have any homosexual tendencies?" he asked and immediately ticked the 'no' box before I had a chance to answer. I was off the hook.

"Ok all done, sign here and then we can get you kitted out. Welcome to the Squadron."

I couldn't believe it. He could have rejected me, but he gave me a chance.

Top Recruit

Sergeant Roberts put us all through the ringer, but he somehow managed to get more out of us than we knew we had to give. They call it the 40% rule. Whenever we were on our chin straps, shaking physically, trying to push out ten more press ups, or struggling up a sand hill with a stretcher full of sandbags, he would shout at us all, "Come on ladies, when you think you're empty, you've got 60% left in the tank!" and he would get that 60% out of us. I never knew what physical reserves I had until then. I was fitter than I had ever been. His faith in me gave me a new found confidence. I would have followed him anywhere.

I went on to do my basic training at the Women's Royal Army Corps barracks in Guildford. Sergeant Roberts had pushed me to the limit of my endurance, so I was well prepared for the training. I even found myself pushing the other girls through the physical as Sergeant Roberts had done for me. I actually enjoyed the training. I was good at it.

I passed out on the 6th October on my 21st birthday. Sergeant Roberts came down to watch the Passing Out parade. After the parade we were led into the chapel where the Commandant sang our praises for making it through training and wished us all well on our return to our units. Then she added, "It is also my pleasure to award the certificate for Top Recruit of 7 Platoon to Private Williams who has just turned twenty-one today."

I went ten shades of crimson and nearly fell off my seat. I marched up, saluted the Commandant, took my certificate and as I turned to smile for the camera, the whole chapel started singing "Happy Birthday to you..." and the canteen staff brought out a cake for me, candles and all. I felt like crying.

Seeing the pride on Sergeant Roberts face was priceless. It was his faith in me that made me believe in myself.

Best birthday present ever...

The following year, Sgt Roberts nominated me for the Junior Non Commissioned Officer cadre for promotion to Lance Corporal. That petrified me. I didn't feel ready. I'd heard horror stories about how physically and mentally demanding the course was. This was the first time females had been allowed on a Royal Engineers Junior NCO cadre and they weren't going to make any exceptions for us. If you couldn't keep up with the guys, you were off the course, simple.

JNCO Cadre

The course was held over two weeks at the navy base HMS Osprey on Portland Bill, Devon. After an eight hour drive we finally settled ourselves into our billets and started getting to know the other nominees on the course who had come from all over the country. There were twenty of us, fifteen blokes and five girls.

The first week consisted of teaching practice. We had to present lessons to the course which consisted of drills, weapon stripping, cleaning and assembling, map reading, field craft and nuclear, chemical and biological warfare. We were all well up into the night preparing our lesson plans, bulling our boots and ironing our kit. I averaged four hours sleep each night. No course since has ever exhausted me like that one. We had to be outside our billets at 5.30am in P.T. kit for the first run of the day.

It was the same story every morning, the Corporals beasting us to tears up 'puke hill'. One hour later we were showered, fed and standing to attention on the parade square for the first drill lesson of the day. My legs were screaming, but we were marched around for at least two hours until everyone had taken a turn at controlling the squad. Then we were off to the classroom to teach which ever lesson we had been given to present. It was a welcome break from all the physical exertion but still nerve wracking because we were being evaluated by the Corporals and Sergeants at the back of the class.

On the second part of the cadre, the navy dropped us off in two Sea King helicopters in the middle of nowhere, with just a map, radio, SA80 rifle and our fully loaded army Bergen. We were out there for five days and four nights during which we averaged three hours broken sleep each night.

On the second day, the support staff unloaded a cage full of live chickens and proceeded to show us how to kill, pluck and cook them for dinner. I wasn't particularly hungry so I decided to pass as a conscientious objector. Sergeant Roberts was not impressed. "Willow, if you don't do this you run the risk of failing the course," he said. I apologised but I just couldn't bring myself to kill a chicken. Considering I already had previous for slaughtering a bunch of crows, the irony wasn't lost on me.

I lead my section into battle three times over the four nights on an empty stomach. On the last day we had a fifteen mile forced march across the moors. We were all on our chin straps. I had nothing left in me. I was running on empty. My knees were on fire and my Bergen had rubbed the skin bare on my lower back. When I saw those army wagons in the distance I nearly cried. It was all over. We were going home. When we got to the wagons, the Corporals shouted over the sound of the engines, "Dig a bit deeper guys, you've got another 10k to go, or you can get on the back of the wagon now. Your choice."

We all looked at each other in disbelief. One of the guys took off his Bergen and threw it onto the back of the wagon.

I looked at Sergeant Roberts. "40% Willow."

Please let me get in the wagon…

I knew I didn't have that option. He gave me a stern look and nodded his head towards the hill. I didn't question him. I just turned and started walking towards the bottom of the hill. My rifle was so heavy and the strap was digging into my neck. I adjusted it for the hike to the top. There were only seventeen of us left from the original twenty that started the course. We all dug in and helped each other up the hill. As we neared the brow of the hill, there was an unmistakeable sound coming from the other side. We got to the top of the hill, and there in the valley 200 metres away was the most beautiful sight I had ever seen. Two Navy Sea King helicopters, and they were waiting for us. I have never in my life felt such a feeling of achievement as when I boarded that helicopter. It was over. I was so close to throwing in the towel, when I was three feet from gold. So many people give up when they are close to succeeding. That was one of the most valuable lessons that I ever had. Sometimes you just can't see what is over the hill. Just keep putting one foot in front of the other; never give up.

I felt so proud to be passing out that day; I couldn't have walked any taller. It was a beautiful sunny day in June as we marched out in front of the Brigade, 300 soldiers, all eyes on us. I wondered which one of the guys would come top and be promoted by the Brigadier.

We all stood to attention and the Brigadier began praising all of our efforts for making it through the extremely demanding course. Then he announced that the best recruit had shown a grit and determination to succeed in the face of injury and adversity and displayed the necessary leadership qualities required of a Junior NCO.

"The award for Best Student of the Junior NCO cadre goes to Private Catherine Williams."

You have got to be joking!

I tried to hide the smile on my face but I couldn't. I marched up to the Brigadier, stood to attention and saluted.

"Well done Willow." He handed me a plaque and a stripe to sew onto my uniform.

Once the parade was over, I got lots of pats on the back and the obligatory photo for the local rag and for the Military edition of Armed Forces which ran a story with the headline, 'First Female tops Royal Engineers Junior NCO cadre.' Which was a definite improvement from my previous headline.

Looking back, I realised that not getting into the Medics was the best thing that could have happened to me, although I felt crushed at the time. I never would have had the same opportunities as I'd had in the Engineers. Some failures can be successes; we just don't see the bigger picture at the time.

Over the next two years, I did a few more courses and also spent some time in Germany as Regimental Signals Instructor after being promoted to Full Corporal. I enjoyed the camaraderie of the Engineers but after six years, I started to get itchy feet. I needed a change. I got chatting to Phil, one of the lads who'd left the unit and joined the police. He actually made it sound like a really good career move. I began wondering if joining the police might be an option. The irony wasn't lost on me but I was starting to enjoy a good challenge.

I applied for Merseyside Police and passed the exam and the fitness test but by the time I got into the interview stage, it was obvious I hadn't done my homework. I didn't even know the Chief Constable's name. I didn't get through.

FAIL

In an effort to get even more comfortable with rejection, I decided to apply for Cheshire Police on a whim. Again, I got as far as the interview but was unsuccessful. The feedback I received was that they did not think I had any particular loyalties or ties to Cheshire, which was true.

FAIL

They could see right through me. I didn't want to be a copper anyway and these rejection letters were really starting to get on my nerves.

My Regiment had just been put on standby to be mobilised for a war I didn't agree with and some of our boys were being flown back from the Gulf in caskets. To top it off, my partner at the time came home and told me she was pregnant and I had a sneaky suspicion it wasn't mine. It made my decision to leave that much easier. I packed my bags and moved to London.

Brothers in Arms

*Playing soldiers was so much fun when David and
John were Ten,
Two little brothers running around shooting each
other over again,
Now they felt they were all grown up although only Seventeen,
John went to join the Infantry and David became
a Royal Marine.*

*Two picture frames on a mantelpiece, pressed uniforms
looking so smart,
Mother & Father beaming with pride, a special place
in both their hearts.
David set sail and John flew out to a war-zone somewhere afar,
With a brotherly hug they said their goodbyes,
first time ever apart.*

In a land far away, they fought for their lives,
knowing it was no longer a game,
Why are we fighting these men just like us?
Underneath we are all the same.
Language and race, religion too, give the illusion
of separateness,
But every time David lifted his gun, all he saw
was his brother's face.

A crack of gunfire filled the air and David felt a pinch
in his chest,
He raised his gun toward the soldier & slowly the
trigger was pressed,
A smell of cordite, a plume of smoke left drifting
amongst the trees,
As it cleared, he could just make out the soldier
falling to his knees.

Their eyes met for a second, and David had never felt so alone,
The face that was looking back at him, he realised was his own,
As the gun fell to the floor the soldier took his final breath,
The dawning realisation he just witnessed his own death.

Mother's boys were coming home, but there would
be no celebrations,
Two HM Service letters promising posthumous commendations,
Together Forever, David and John playing soldiers
amongst the stars.
Two caskets draped in Union Flags, Forever Brothers In Arms…

- Fear of failure is simply a fear of rejection. Get comfortable with the discomfort.

- Failure makes future success more meaningful. The more obstacles we have to overcome to achieve our goal, the greater the satisfaction.

- The cost of succumbing to fear is a mediocre life, filled with regret.

- When you think you're empty, you've still got 60% in the tank.

- Persistence is key. Most people give up when they're just three feet from gold.

The Metropolitan Police

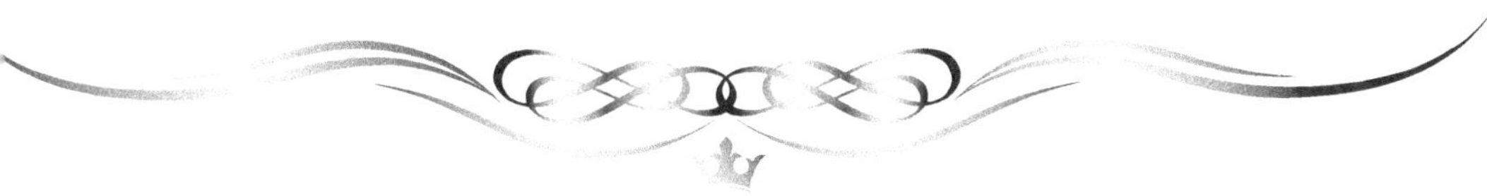

Chapter 5

The Metropolitan Police

"To maintain at all times a relationship with the public that gives reality to the historic tradition that the police are the public and that the public are the police."

Sir Robert PEEL

A few weeks after arriving in London, those brick walls started to weigh on my mind like unfinished business. I decided to apply for the Metropolitan Police. The application asked if I had ever been convicted of an offence. I thought about the question for a while before answering. I hadn't been convicted of an offence but I was certainly guilty of one. But it hadn't asked whether I had ever been on a drunken rampage and become airborne in a stolen vehicle. I ticked the NO box.

A few weeks went by and when I didn't hear anything, I convinced myself that Scotland Yard had found out all about my sordid past. I decided to confess to the Superintendent of recruitment and training. My confession outlined the whole joyriding incident in full technicolour detail along with a heartfelt plea for leniency.

When I got back from the post office, there was an envelope with the Met logo on it sitting on the mat.

You must be joking...

It read, 'Dear Catherine, we are pleased to invite you for an interview on the 13th September.'

I sat quietly on the stairs for the next fifteen minutes staring at the Met logo and contemplating exactly what part of my DNA was hell bent on self-destruction.

Judas!

Two days later I rang the recruitment branch. They confirmed they had received my signed confession and went on to say that my application had been suspended pending a Superintendent's decision. It was the longest week of my life. By the following Friday, I received a follow up letter telling me to come on the original date for interview. I couldn't believe it.

I spent the next few weeks reading all the broadsheets and doing as much research on the Met as I possibly could. The morning of the interview I popped to the newsagents for a bottle of water. Something told me to buy a copy of the Guardian newspaper. I'm not sure why. I felt I'd done enough swatting. If I didn't know it now I never would. I bought a copy anyway and read it on the tube.

I arrived at the Recruitment Branch half an hour early, all suited and booted. I was nervous, but I also felt quietly confident. I'd had weeks to prepare for the interview. There were about fifteen people in the waiting room and four interview rooms. I barely had time to introduce myself to the guy sitting next to me when my name was called.

"Catherine Williams?"

"That's me," I said. My heart started pounding in my chest. I took a deep breath, walked in and gave the panel a big smile. There were three interviewers, a civilian personnel officer from Human Resources, a Sergeant and an Inspector. Seated behind them was a man I recognised straight away from reading the Police Federation newspaper. His name was John Barney, the Federation Secretary. I was told Mr Barney was a neutral observer during the interview.

The Sergeant was the first to open up the interview after the introductions.

"Ok Catherine, first thing's first," he said with a grin that he was trying to hide behind his beard. "Tell me about the fork lift truck."

He had my hand written confession in front of him on the table. I couldn't help but smile. "Sir, all I can say is I was young and foolish. My solicitor called it hi-jinx."

"But you never received a conviction despite pleading guilty?" asked the Inspector.

"No sir, the case was dismissed," I said.

The Inspector started to laugh and so did the rest of the panel. "Incredible. What is the legal system coming to when we can't even get a conviction when someone pleads guilty?" he said.

The whole panel were laughing now including John Barney, who was laughing in a neutral kind of way without looking up from his notes. I wanted to laugh but I thought it was inappropriate so I sat there with an inane grin on my face until the interview started proper.

"Ok Catherine, the French have been carrying out nuclear tests in the aurora atoll recently. How do you think that might affect us here in London?" asked the Inspector.

As luck would have it, the Guardian was running a piece about the tests in that morning's paper. "Well sir, there is a lot of objection from environmentalists to the testing and this could result in protests outside the French Embassy in Knightsbridge."

What a stroke of luck. I hadn't even known where the French Embassy was thirty minutes before.

"Do you think cannabis should be legalised?" I couldn't believe it. Page 10 Guardian Comment was also running a story on legalising cannabis. I was able to give a reasonable argument for and against.

Too easy.

Almost every question was straight from that morning's Guardian. It was a god send. All that swatting had given me an air of confidence though which I hadn't had in the previous two interviews. The last question was "Is honesty always the best policy?"

"I think I'll be better able to answer that question when I get my interview result, sir." I smiled.

It felt like an hour but I was only in there for 25 minutes. I wasn't sure whether that was good or bad. I was told to go back to the waiting room with the other candidates.

The personnel officer called me in to the office and asked, "Do you want the good news or the bad news?" My heart sank.

"The bad news," I said.

"There isn't any, you passed," he said. I reckon he never tired of that bit of fun. He could see the relief on my face as I burst out laughing. I wanted to kiss him.

"The panel admired your integrity," he said. "Your confession probably swung that interview in your favour."

I couldn't believe it. Maybe honesty was the best policy after all. I left there walking a little taller that day. I smiled all the way home.

Metropolitan Police Training School – Hendon

On Sunday the 14th April 1996, I found myself standing outside the gates of the Metropolitan Police Training Centre in Hendon, North London. I felt like a total fraud.

I don't belong here.

I approached the gatehouse where a friendly Metropolitan police member from the security staff gave me a welcoming smile and asked for my I.D. "Don't look so nervous," he said. "It's only five months."

He'd probably seen hundreds of nervous faces walk through those gates. He found my name on a long list and ticked it off and then gave me directions to the accommodation blocks.

I found my way to North Tower where I was checked in and given a key to my room. The rooms were comfortable and functional. They had a single bed, a desk to study at, a fitted wardrobe and a sink.

Over the course of the morning, new recruits started to arrive in dribs and drabs. Proud parents were helping carry suitcases, duvets and

fluffy pillows upstairs for these future keepers of the Queen's Peace. It reminded me a little of my first day at boarding school only more truncheons and less hockey sticks.

Judging by the tearful departures, some of these prospective Sheriffs had clearly never spent a night away from home in the whole of their very sheltered lives.

Toughen up princess…

Finally, when all the parents had left, we were able to introduce ourselves. My next door neighbour was a very loud Scottish girl called Pamela. She was a friendly type, very extroverted. Definitely no wall flower. On the other side of Pamela was Wendy. She was from Liverpool and as soon as I heard the accent, I knew we'd hit it off straight away. She came across as quite reserved but she had a typical scouse dry sense of humour.

We had all been given instructions to head over to Simpson Hall at 2.00pm. I walked over with Pamela and Wendy. We took our seats and shortly after the Head of Training took the stage and welcomed Green Intake of 1996 to The Metropolitan Police Training School.

There were 130 recruits split into six individual classes. The staff carried out a role call and we were all assigned our classrooms for the next day. I was in 'B' Class with Pam and Wendy. We were then introduced to our friendly instructors for the next twenty weeks. The Assistant Commissioner then welcomed us to the Metropolitan Police family and we were all sworn in together. He then gave us a little motivational spiel that I'm sure he gave to each intake.

"Welcome Green Intake of 96. You are now members of the finest and most professional police force in the world. We lead, others follow.

Remember what an enormous responsibility you are undertaking serving the people of London. Do not abuse that authority. Each one you is a representative of the whole and I expect the same standards of you both on and off duty. Policing is an enormously fulfilling job and I wish each and every one of you all the success in your careers."

Bristling with pride, we all went to sign our lives away in the Warrant Book. The book had hundreds of Metropolitan Police officer's signatures going back years. My warrant was 197224.

I was now officially Police Constable Catherine Williams 197224. My joyriding days were over.

Over the course of the following few weeks, the staff moulded us into London's finest Metropolitan Police officers. We underwent inspections each morning. Our uniform had to be immaculately pressed and if the Drill Sergeant couldn't see his face in the toe caps of your boots, he'd

march us around for an extra hour. We marched everywhere. We had drill practice four times a week to get us ready for our Passing Out Parade and we were being regularly tortured by the P.T. staff in order to get us into peak physical condition.

There were exams every Monday and Friday and we were expected to know all the legislation by rote. If you failed an exam you could be back-classed five weeks to the following intake. That meant staying at Hendon an extra five weeks and passing out with a different intake. That was everyone's worst nightmare.

Our instructor, Ross aka 'Charisma', came and told us our postings had been published and were on the wall outside the staff room. We all ran down and huddled around the board like a group of exam students looking for our grades. I scanned the names, mine was at the bottom. Police Constable Catherine Williams 197224 AB Belgravia Division.

Where the hell is Belgravia?

I'd never even heard of the place.

It felt like a life time but the 16th August finally came around and 'B' Class, Green Intake of 1996 'Legends in their own Lunch Time' passed out with all the fanfare. I looked at myself in the mirror and realised that I had become a police officer.

I felt like I'd changed so much in those few months. I had walked through those gates feeling like a fraud and now I was walking out with my warrant in my back pocket as so many had done before me. I felt proud that I had passed the training and surprisingly, I actually wanted to serve the people of London without fear or favour, malice or ill will.

What have they done to me?

Somehow they had instilled a sense of pride and belonging. Who would have thought?

Proud Dad

Puppy Walking

I turned up at Belgravia Police Station on the first day feeling extremely nervous. There were eight of us on the eleven-week long street duties course. We were posted with experienced police officers who took us out on the beat and volunteered us for the worst jobs they could find. It was affectionately called 'puppy walking'.

It felt strange walking around London in uniform. Everybody watches you. It's definitely a spectator sport. I never ventured far from the safety and security of my street duties instructor's bosom. My first morning I was posted with Al. He had about ten years on the job and was still very keen. We were walking past Victoria coach station when Al pointed at a black hackney cab that was parked up on the zigzag hazard lines

approaching the pedestrian crossing.

"Go get 'em tiger!" he said.

I started to walk towards the black cab nervously. Al followed close behind and stood about ten feet away.

"Morning sir. You're parked on the hazard lines. You can't park here," I said.

"Yeah, alright darlin' I was just dropping off. I'm going now," he said.

"Do you have your licence on you sir?"

"Of course I don't! It's in the cab innit? You a rookie or sunnink?"

"Sir, I'm going to issue you with a Fixed Penalty Notice for parking on the hazard lines. It's three points and a £60 fine," I said while flicking through the codes on my FPN book.

"You have got to be fricking joking? I was just dropping off," he said throwing his hands in the air.

By this time Al had sidled over to the cabbie. "Alright mate. Got your bill and badge on you?"

The cabbie leant into the cab and showed Al his 'bill and badge' which they are obliged to carry. His bill is the license mounted in the cab and his badge he is supposed to wear at all times.

Al showed me where the cabbies license was all nicely mounted in the back where the passengers could see it.

"I knew it. I'm getting a friggin' ticket cos she's a rookie!" he said.

I issued him with the ticket and he drove away shouting out of the window as he went. Dealing with black cab drivers was always confrontational so it was a good place to start building up that thick skin. You invariably got a court date out of it too. The cabbie would turn up in court with ten of his cabbie mates who had all co-incidentally been in the street at the time of the alleged offence. Under oath they would perjure themselves to bail their fellow cabbie out.

"Your worship, I seen Reggie's cab stop yeah, but that's cos his fare opened the back door. He dint 'av no choice your worshipness."

My first arrest wasn't much better. I arrested a vagrant shoplifter and then I got all my times and facts mixed up while I was giving my evidence to the custody Sergeant. He just rolled his eyes at 'Paddy the vagrant' who laughed and with his whisky infused broad Irish accent asked, "You a rookie then? Would ya loike me to tell the good Sergeant what happened dear? Roight, oy made me way in to Woollies where oy proceeded to put a ham and cheese sarnie down the front of me trousers, your honour!"

He was laughing so much he almost fell off the bench.

"Thanks Paddy, anything else you want to add?" I asked.

"Yes, oym innocent. You planted that sarnie in me trousers!" and he fell about laughing again.

Paddy was no stranger to Belgravia police station and he knew that he would have a bed for the night and a free meal. It was better than being on the street.

Towards the end of the street duties course, we were finally let out on

our own to wreak havoc on the travelling public with a pocket full of Fixed Penalty Notices. We survived the street duties course and were each posted to our respective teams.

We underwent continuation training regularly during our probation to keep us all up to date on the most pressing issues such as Equal Opportunities and Diversity. Now I'm all for equal ops, but not at the expense of common sense and effective leadership. As we were all to find out, The Met was the most politically correct animal we would ever encounter. God forbid we ever uttered a sentence that might offend someone. Anyone.

Political Correctness Gone Mad

During large occasions such as Trooping the Colour for the Queen's birthday or State visits, the Met opened up its feeding centre in Buckingham Gate. It always reminded me of the Tardis in Doctor Who. From the front, it was an unassuming Victorian terrace, yet a never ending stream of police officers disappeared through its doors each morning only to appear an hour later fed and watered by the Met's finest canteen staff.

The feeding centre was a real melting pot of differing rank and file officers. Some from Specialist Operations units like SO19 Specialist Firearms or the Territorial Support Group who deal with public order situations, SO16 Diplomatic Protection officers, but most were salt of the earth, good for a laugh, general duties beat bobbies. I enjoyed going there because I always caught up with mates I hadn't seen for ages and had a good old banter.

We were corralled into the dining area by the canteen staff until the queue snaked around the outside wall of the room. Hanging on every coat hook at the back of the room were bobbies' helmets, jackets and utility belts. It felt a little like being back at primary school.

We weren't allowed to choose where we sat either. The canteen staff put us in our seats in the order we came off the line. There was always a certain amount of sulking and big bottom lips when the canteen staff split up guys on the same unit but their word was final. You could see some guys nervously counting how many seats were left on the next table and moving back in the queue so they didn't end up being the only Safer Neighbourhoods P.C. sat with a bunch of knuckle dragging Territorial Support Group P.C.'s. Anyone would think we were standing in the prison line at Alcatraz, not the Metropolitan Police feeding centre.

Whenever someone is promoted to 'Skipper' (Met speak for Sergeant) or a 'Guvnor' (Met speak for Inspector) being issued with their pips and stripes gives them an uncanny ability to disappear into thin air at a moment's notice.

You could empty any Met canteen of all Inspectors and Sergeants simply by the mere suggestion that something politically incorrect was about to happen. On a long day it kept us amused for hours. The quickest I ever saw the feeding centre empty though was when my mate Shazza, who I hadn't seen in a while, affectionately shouted across the hall "Look at the fat arse on that lezza!" in a broad cockney accent.

"Fat arse lezza", understandably, is not politically correct. Now it didn't matter that I personally wasn't offended by this remark, because someone else can be offended on my behalf. How fantastic. I don't even have to be in the room and someone else can willingly take offence for me. Offence by proxy.

It was the general consensus that if you were so easily offended then you were probably in the wrong job. It is a supervisor's duty and responsibility to challenge such politically incorrect, divisive and abusive remarks.

And if they decide not to challenge them, then they'd better make damn sure they were never within ear shot or they're screwed. The police terminology for such a situation is "He was upstairs collecting fares", which is a throwback from the old double decker buses. It meant he was engaged elsewhere, not within earshot and could not possibly have challenged an exchange he did not hear. Guvnors were upstairs collecting fares a lot.

Eventually the P.C. environment killed off a lot of the canteen banter and we were banned from even using nicknames for fear of upsetting someone. That caused some confusion because no-one knew what Gripper, Foetus and Token's real names were.

I managed to get through my probation without offending too many wall flowers and found myself sitting in the Superintendent's office shaking his hand.

"Good morning Cath. Well, congratulations. You've passed your probation."

"Thank you sir."

"Let me ask you, what is your opinion of the division's policy of single manning?"

"To be honest sir, I'm not a fan."

"Well, it's our way of spreading the jam that bit thinner."

"Well, I think it's an officer safety issue, sir."

"Really? Well statistically speaking, your likelihood of being assaulted on this division is once every twelve years," he said.

I couldn't help but think that those odds were significantly reduced if you were sitting in an office surrounded by 12 inch thick walls.

"Well, sir, I've been on the division two years and I've already had my ribs and my nose broken," I said.

[Pause]

"Well, anyway, well done Cath, see Judy on the way out, she's got your certificate."

Cheers Boss...

Chapter 6

The Knock At The Door

Chapter 6

The Knock At The Door

"Life is so beautiful that death has fallen in love with it, a jealous, possessive love that grabs at what it can."

Yann Martel, Life of Pi

One thing you have to get used to dealing with as a police officer is death. It certainly gives you an appreciation for how fragile life can be. On each team there always seems to be one person who gets more than their fair share of sudden deaths. On our team, that was my friend Lynda or as we liked to call her, 'Dr. Death.'

Lynda had about seven years service when I joined the team, so I would go to her for advice but it always came with a side helping of sarcasm and quick witted insult. Lynda was our resident artist and when she wasn't drawing caricatures of people she disliked on the control room white board, she could be found rushing around the corridors with an empty file in her hand looking busy. I wanted to be just like her, dodging the shit jobs, while maintaining an air of responsibility.

Lynda was like a mentor to me, and by that, I don't mean she taught me all I know about police work. I mean she showed me all the best coffee shops and hidey holes around Westminster. Unfortunately, when Lynda was transferred to another station, she passed her title on to me. The

control room was inundated with sudden deaths and despite me rushing around the corridors with an empty file in my hand, it didn't wash. The 'empty file' tactic was good for avoiding juvenile shoplifters and drunks but it wouldn't get you out of dealing with a sudden death. I didn't mind them to be honest. I'd rather deal with a corpse than a teenager with attitude any day.

One thing I never got used to though was having to tell someone that a friend or family member had died.

Death Messages

There is no easy way to tell someone that a loved one is not coming home. All the scenario based training won't help when you're faced with such an outpouring of grief. My first death message did not go at all by the book. The book says take them inside the house, sit them down, if possible make sure they have someone with them. Don't use the word accident. Be compassionate.

It was an awful feeling knowing I was about to give someone news that would change their life forever. We join the job wanting to help people, not turn their life upside down.

I arrived on the doorstep just as the lady was coming out of her house.

"Are you Mrs. Audrey Jones?"

"Yes. Why? What's happened?"

"Can we go inside Mrs. Jones?"

"No. tell me now. What's happened? Is it Bill?"

The look of fear in her eyes was too much.

"I'm very sorry Mrs. Jones. There has been an accident. Bill was hit by a car."

"Is he ok. Please tell me he's ok."

"I am so sorry. He died from his injuries. There was nothing they could do."

She collapsed on the front door step.

Bill had literally popped out to the shop on his bike to get a pint of milk as he did most days, only today he never came home. How does anyone make sense of that?

I stayed and comforted her until her sister arrived and then before I had time to process things, I was sent to deal with a domestic dispute between two people arguing over a remote control.

Seriously?

"So what was the fight about then?" I asked.

"I was watching Eastenders and she just threw the remote at me 'ead!"

"Ok, so no-one's dead then?" I asked.

"Of course not. What you on about?"

"Why have you called the police?"

"She threw a REMOTE at me 'ead! I wan' her charged!"

Oh for f…

"Why don't you both grow up!"

"Wha'? You can't talk to me like that!"

"Yeah, you can't talk to him like that," piped up the woman who had just bounced the remote off his head.

"I just did. Now stop wasting everyone's time or you'll both be getting locked up."

"We pay your wages you know!"

"Yeah, I'll have your badge officer!"

Having a common enemy seemed to help them patch up their differences though so all was not lost. They were still shouting from the balcony as we drove off and I could not have cared less. My thoughts were with Mrs. Jones.

Soho Bombing Casualty Bureau

Whenever there is a large scale emergency such as a rail crash or a bombing involving numerous victims, the Met set up a Casualty bureau. The number is broadcast on the television and hundreds of officers are drafted in to man the phones, attend relative's addresses etc. I was drafted in for both the Paddington rail crash and the Soho bombing. It was our job to gather as much information as possible and when we were sure that the caller's loved one had been identified, we would dispatch two officers to their house.

When The Admiral Duncan gay bar in Soho was blown up, I was answering the phones when I received a call from a worried Irish mother.

"Good morning dear. I think my son may have been exploded in that Captain Drunken pub."

"You mean the Admiral Duncan pub ma'am? And why do you think that?"

"Well dear, he lives in London and he's, you know… gay."

"I see. Well, have you tried to call him?"

"Oh no dear. We haven't spoken for four years since his father kicked him out."

"So maybe you should try and call him to see if he's ok."

"Well I wouldn't know what to say dear."

"How about, I'm glad you haven't been exploded, when are you coming home?"

"Oh his father would never agree to that dear."

She was amongst many mothers who called to check on their exiled sons. I had no idea how many gay boys got kicked out of home by their families. It was quite sad.

First Sudden Death

I dealt with my first sudden death during my probation. It was at an apartment block called Dolphin Square in Pimlico. I was with an experienced P.C. but I was still nervous as hell. I'd never even seen a dead body before.

When we arrived, The London Ambulance Service (LAS) were already there. They were all gloved up and with a smile one of the crew said, "You here for the purple?"

"Why's he talking about purple, Steve? What's a purple?" I asked nervously.

Steve just laughed. "Don't worry about the purple, it's the purple plus you wanna worry about."

The LAS guy must have noticed my shiny new boots. "First sudden death love'? Don't' worry, he aint that bad."

The LAS grade the sudden deaths depending on how long and how decomposed they are, i.e. purple and purple plus. In the scheme of things, this guy wasn't too bad. He was a Member of Parliament and the reason he had been found was because there had been a division in the house and all MP's had been called in to vote. This is the one time that Metropolitan police officers are obliged to assist the MP in getting to the Houses of Parliament by whichever means possible. This could include stopping traffic to allow the MP right of way, and believe it or not, even using the bus lane.

Sacrilege!

When I entered the apartment and saw this poor chap laying face down on his floor naked, on top of a Cornish pasty, I was pretty sure we weren't going to get him there in time for the vote. What surprised me though, was that the person who found him was another MP and he didn't think it important enough to call the police until after the vote, and even then it appeared to be an afterthought. I can only imagine the conversation…

"Damn and blast! The old bugger's stiff as a board."

"Well can't you just prop him up old chap? No-one will notice."

"How bloody inconvenient. We needed that vote."

'Ah well, looks like there's an opening at the country club if you're still interested James?"

Maria the 23-year-old Italian Student

One afternoon shift, I was working with Chris when we received a call to attend an accident in Buckingham Palace Road, 'Bus versus Pedestrian' as the control room put it. It sounded quite serious so every available car was dispatched. I jumped out of the car and grabbed the first aid bag from the boot and headed over to where everyone was standing. As I approached the bus lane, I could see water running down the curb and into the gutter, but I couldn't work out where it was coming from. I went to step over it and it began to glisten crimson red under the street lighting. Even then it took a few more seconds for me to realise what I was looking at. There was just so much of it. It literally stopped me in my tracks.

We can't fix this...

There were five officers leaning over someone in the bus lane. No-one was speaking. I knew then that whatever I was about to see was going to leave its mark. You can't unsee things, can you? I took a deep breath and leant down next to one of the guys. The poor girl was unrecognisable. She was lying there motionless and one of the officers was trying to take a pulse but all I could think was how can she have a pulse if the top of her head is gone? I know now that she was doing it more to reassure the public than anything else.

She's gone...

There is a world of difference between attending a sudden death where someone has been dead for a while and attending an incident where someone has just been killed. I had never seen anything like this.

　　　www.CatWilliamz.com

The ambulance crew arrived shortly after and looked her over. The younger of the two seemed quite shaken up. "This is my first fatal," he said.

"Mine too," I replied.

A passing doctor came over and asked, "Would you like me to pronounce her?"

"Yes please doctor," I said.

"Pronounced life extinct at 7.40pm. Here's my card." And he walked off to the train station. All in a days' work. As simple as that. Those two little words. Life extinct.

Is that it?

Here one minute and gone the next. I spent the next two hours on a cordon deep in thought, while the crash examiner started his investigation. He said it was the worst he had seen in twenty-five years. She lay there under a sheet in the gutter until they had finished taking photographs and measuring the scene.

The longer she lay there, the more frustrated I was getting. We still didn't know who she was and all I could think was, someone, somewhere is waiting for her to come home. Their life is about to be turned upside down by a knock at the door and they don't even know. An overwhelming sadness came over me which I was rudely shaken out of by Mr "Police cordons don't apply to me" Smith. He lifted up the police tape and proceeded to walk towards the train station.

"Where the hell do you think you're going pal?" I shouted.

"I'm going to miss my train, officer," he replied and continued walking, briefcase in hand. I grabbed hold of his shirt sleeve and pulled him towards the tape.

"Don't touch me," he said and tried to shake his arm free. "This is just another bloody knee jerk reaction to an empty suitcase, I'll bet!"

"This isn't a bomb scare mate," I said as I deposited him back outside the cordon. "There's a dead girl lying in the middle of the street over there. Do you want to tell her parents she's not coming home? Now piss off!" I shouted at him.

My Inspector, having seen all this, started to walk over. Mr Smith was looking a little shocked.

"Everything alright, sir?" Inspector Neal asked in his broad Scottish accent.

"This officer just told me to piss off," he replied.

"Did she now? Best you do then," said Inspector Neal.

"Best I do what?" asked Mr Smith

"Piss off!" replied Inspector Neal.

Mr. Smith, now open mouthed and looking completely horrified, finally took the hint and pissed off.

"Cheers Guv. I know I shouldn't have sworn at him," I said.

"Aye, you should. He was a tosser," he said and he patted me on the back and told me to keep up the good work. That meant a lot to me. He was one of those supervisors you would follow into battle. He really looked after his troops.

We found out her name was Maria. She was a twenty-three year old Italian student who lived with her boyfriend south of the river. My heart went out to him but I was glad not to be the one knocking on his door that night. When we finished the shift, Inspector Neal ordered everyone to the 'Sundial', the local pub for a debrief. He went round and chatted to everyone individually. It was his way of making sure everyone was ok. He wouldn't let you leave until he'd managed to get you to crack a smile. He was priceless.

Jenny the 26-year-old Shop Assistant

I was working one night shift with Marco when a call came in for a unit to deal with a female with head injuries in Churchill Gardens estate. When we arrived, I was surprised to see her lying there alone at the bottom of one of the high rises. There was no-one else around. No-one even attempting to give her first aid. I could see a few people on the balconies above looking over, maybe they had called it in but hadn't wanted to get involved.

She wasn't moving. I checked for a pulse. Nothing. I lifted her eyelids. Her pupils were fixed.

"She's dead Marco."

I'd watched people being fished out of the Thames and stood at hospital beds and seen a young girl have her stomach pumped, but this was the first successful suicide I'd seen. I was relieved to see a sea of flashing blue lights heading towards us as the rest of the team started turning up. This brought people out onto their balconies in their nightgowns to see what had happened. I stayed with the body while Marco arranged for forensics, scene examiner and Duty Inspector to attend.

I was relieved once we got the forensic tent over her. I hated that everyone could see her lying there. Death can be so undignified but it was her choice to end her life right here in full view of everyone on the estate. I searched her clothing for I.D. wondering who she was and what had brought her to this. I moved her hand from her side to reach into her pockets. It was cold, clammy and lifeless.

Twenty minutes earlier these hands had held the railings of the fifteenth floor before she let go and fell away from the building, into the darkness without so much as a sound. Resolute. No turning back. No-one saw her fall past their window. No-one heard her scream. It was only the sound of flesh against concrete that brought people to their front doors to see what was going on. I could only imagine the total despair she must have felt in her final moments.

"When you look into the Abyss, the Abyss is looking into you."

Nietzsche

The coroner's verdict stated Jenny had committed suicide. Her diary was a sad indictment of everything that is wrong with our society, or rather our expectations as a society. Jenny lived alone. She was single and slightly overweight. She had been on a few dates but nothing had worked out. With each rejection her self-loathing grew. Her diary was filled with shame and self-hatred. She couldn't quiet that voice inside her head that kept telling her she wasn't good enough, she wasn't pretty enough, slim enough. The voice that told her she would always be alone because she was ugly and unlovable.

To quote Brene Brown, author of 'Gifts of Imperfection', shame needs three things to survive; secrecy, silence and judgement. Jenny had all that and more. Shame forced her to climb over that balcony. I wondered if one word of comfort or a smile from a stranger may have made a difference that night.

The Abyss

Standing on the edge of the great Abyss,
It wasn't supposed to feel like this.
Arms outstretched I fall through space,
Into the void, this soulless place.

Lost and alone, darkness blinding my sight,
No escape from this torturous absence of light.
Mocked by shadows in the deep of the night.
Trying to run but my feet are stuck tight.

The emptiness stealing the air that I breathe.
Desolate, barren prison, no hope of reprieve.
Sentenced to life in this black chasm gaol,
Or pardoned by the hammer and iron casket nail.

Too afraid to keep living, and too scared to die,
Tormented in limbo, no tears left to cry.
For what is this life without joy or laughter?
No fairy tale ending, no happy ever after.

Descent into nowhere, this spiraling despair.
This worthless life, with no-one to share.
Death's warm embrace, a comfort from this hell,
For what have I left to lose, but this lifeless empty shell?

Ben the 22-year-old Would Be Poet

Eckhart Tolle describes addiction as unconscious refusal to face and move through your own pain. Every addiction starts with pain and ends with pain. Whatever the substance you are addicted to, you are using something or somebody to cover up your pain.

I was working an early turn and we received a call to attend a drug overdose. When we arrived the ambulance crew were still there. The young man's name was Ben. He was twenty-two and still living at home. His parents were sitting at the kitchen table. I will never forget the look on his mum's face. She was broken. I can't even begin to understand how a mother buries her child.

Ben wasn't from a bad family or unemployed or homeless. He was loved very much and his family had all stood by him while he had tried to get off the gear. One night as his parents were getting ready for bed, he penned them a letter apologising for letting them down and asking their forgiveness. He enclosed a poem for his sister. He couldn't go on. Imagine a life without colour, without joy, without hope, where your first waking thought is 'Where will I get my next fix?' His life was without meaning. The drugs had literally sucked his soul right out of him. He felt there was only one way out of the hell.

At 7.00am the next morning his father went to wake him and found him slumped over his bed with a needle in his arm. He was no longer that beautiful boy in the family photo, full of hope with his whole life ahead of him. But this is the last memory they will have of him. What do you say to them?

I have no words…

Sorry just wasn't enough. Their lives will never be the same.

Young Ben was filled with shame because he had been unable to get off the drugs despite his parents sending him to rehab and giving him all the love and support they could. He still felt they would be better off without him. If he could have foreseen the sheer devastation his death caused the family, I wonder if he would have reconsidered. Shame is like a wound that is never exposed so it never heals.

The Coroner recorded an open verdict as they often do in suicide cases, because even after death, suicide carries such shame and stigma for family members. Most people who kill themselves, they think they're ending the pain, but all they're doing is passing it on to those they leave behind.

The First Bite

The devil may tempt you, but it's always your choice,
He will plant that seed with an Angels voice.
Whispering sweet delights and unfathomable pleasure,
But first you must give up all that you most treasure.

Euphoria gives way to all good intentions,
You're now riding a wave of ecstatic sensations.
As you dance with the devil, cheek to cheek,
You forfeit your soul for the pleasure you seek.

The first bite tastes sweeter than you've ever known,
The devil now Crowned, he sits on his throne.
He knows you'll be back time and again,
You can Chase the Dragon, but it won't feel the same.

The dance now over, you begin the descent,
Never felt so good, don't want it to end...
The darkness envelopes you, as you lay on your bed,
A feeling so dreadful, you may wish yourself dead.

Savour that first bite, as you'll certainly be shown,
You can't crave a feeling you've never known.
A craving so deep you no longer feel whole,
An empty crevice where once sat your soul.

Spend your whole life, feeling something's now missing,
Into someone else's ear your lover's now whispering,
If the devil seduces you and think you just might,
Think twice before you take that First Bite...

- Tell your loved ones that you love them.

- Don't let the sun set on an argument.

- Be nice to everyone you meet. Kindness costs nothing, but it's priceless.

- Shame is the fear that we aren't good enough. Everyone has a right to be here. We are all enough.

Royalty Protection

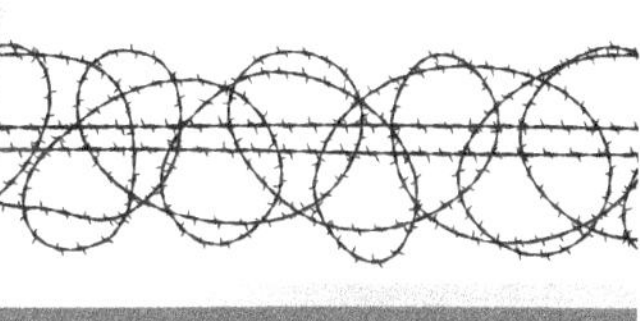

Chapter 7

Royalty Protection

"The world is not the most pleasant place. Eventually your parents leave you and nobody is going to go out of their way to protect you unconditionally."

Queen Elizabeth II

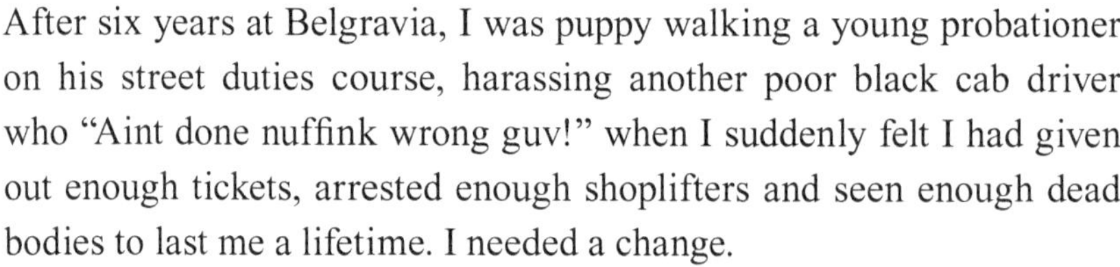

After six years at Belgravia, I was puppy walking a young probationer on his street duties course, harassing another poor black cab driver who "Aint done nuffink wrong guv!" when I suddenly felt I had given out enough tickets, arrested enough shoplifters and seen enough dead bodies to last me a lifetime. I needed a change.

I noticed an ad for the Royalty Protection Department (SO14) as an Authorised Firearms Officer (AFO), so I applied. The security vetting procedure was an extremely involved and lengthy process. I had to undergo psychometric testing, pass the AFO fitness test and sit a final board. I was successful and after passing the board I was offered a conditional appointment working at Buckingham Palace. I had to undergo and pass the three week AFO course at Lippett's Hill, run by SO19 the Met's Specialist Firearms unit.

Authorised Firearms Officer Course

The firearms course was definitely a great leveller. It was an extremely intense course and SO19 take no prisoners. The failure rate was extremely high. On the first day we were introduced to our four very staunch looking SO19 instructors. There were only about fifteen of us on the course, of which two were females. They kept the numbers down so each officer could be assessed thoroughly by their instructor. This was the most disciplined environment that I had been in since joining the Met. I felt at home with that.

We were under constant scrutiny and if we failed any aspect of the course, we were out. They don't care what job you've been promised. My tactic was to volunteer for everything, so what I may have lacked in brawn, I made up for in enthusiasm. They don't want shrinking violets on firearms courses and as a female you have to be twice as assertive to be considered half as good. There was method in my madness though, because the firearms scenarios got progressively harder during the course. I knew I'd cracked it on week two, when I volunteered to lead a building search for an armed suspect and the instructors told me to put my hand down. There's a fine line between being enthusiastic and looking like a brown nose. They picked someone who had up until that point, blended into the background. There is no place to hide on the AFO course.

I passed the course and was given a start date of May 2002. The whole process had taken almost a year.

Toothless Tigers

The first week at the Palace was an eye opener. I soon learnt that as far as the Royal household goes, the police were definitely at the bottom of the food chain. As I made my way through the garden one afternoon, I heard someone frantically shouting "OFFICER! OFFICER!" I spun around ready and eager to offer my assistance to the person in need.

"OFFICER! WHY ARE YOU WALKING ON MY BORDERS!?" It was the gardener.

Who the hell do you think you're talking to pal?

I had committed the heinous crime of 'wanton and carelessly' walking along Her Majesty's lawn edges instead of using the dusty gravel path. The fact that I had just polished my boots held little weight with my furious Royal gardener. I spent the next two minutes being talked down to by a guy with a hoover bag strapped to his back.

Once he'd finished with me, he turned his little hoover bag back on and carried on sucking goose shit up off the lawn. I was now taking orders from a guy who hoovers shit off a lawn for a living. If we'd been on the other side of that garden wall, I'm sure he would have spoken to me with a little more respect, but inside these walls I had become an impotent, toothless tiger. We were a necessary evil and we were tolerated, but not particularly welcome.

It was Golden Jubilee year too so we were extremely busy with Party at the Palace and Trooping the Colour. I was on the search team during that time mainly dealing with all the celebrities coming into the Palace for the party. If I never see the engine of another Bentley again, it will be too soon.

An elderly gentleman approached the gate followed closely by his wife.

"Good morning sir, can I see your I.D. and invite, please?" I asked.

He seemed a little confused by the question, so his wife answered for him.

"This is Dr Buzz Aldrin, first man on the moon," she said.

"That's lovely madam. Do you have your photo I.D. and invite handy?"

"No, I do not. This is Dr Buzz Aldrin, the first man on the moon," she said again. I wasn't sure Neil Armstrong would agree but nevertheless.

Clearly Buzz Aldrin is recognised all over the States but I didn't know him from a bar of soap.

"Sir, do you have any photographic I.D. on you at all?" I asked him. He reached into his jacket and pulled out a Texas driver's license with his picture on it. They had left their invites in the hotel so I escorted them to the Quad and handed them over to one of the Paige's.

To tell you the truth, I was a little in awe of meeting Buzz Aldrin because he is so iconic, but by the time we reached the Quad, I'd heard the word moon seventeen times in one sentence and I was over it.

The Baked Bean

Although I am patriotic, I don't consider myself a Royalist per se, but I challenge even the most hardened anti-monarchist to meet the Queen and not be slightly awed. My first encounter wasn't exactly my finest moment. Her Majesty the Queen of England, who I had sworn to protect, sneaked up on me in the garden, which theoretically she shouldn't be able to do. I mean, if you read the papers, SO14 officers are highly trained elite killing machines. Well, this highly trained elite killing machine was in the middle of writing a poem on the back of an envelope. I was staring into space with my pen in my mouth when I heard, "Officer!"

Here we go...

I turned around expecting to come face to face with another furious gardener.

Oh...

It was the Queen. I shouldn't have been so surprised really, it was her garden.

"Good morning your Majesty. How can I help?" I asked nervously

"Officer, what are those workmen doing in my summerhouse?" she asked.

I suddenly felt like I was back at Goudhurst being scolded by Miss Barbara. The Queen was always preceded by nine yappy type dogs. They were like fool-proof warning beacons.

Where are the bloody dogs?

"I'll find out how long they'll be, ma'am," and I scurried off to the summerhouse.

The workmen had been caught with their feet up on the Queen's garden furniture and now they were too afraid to come out. They were working on the alarms in another part of the garden, but they had decided to take a break in the summer house before knocking off.

"Jesus Christ darlin' she scared the crap out of us," one of them said.

"There's a story for the Grandkids," I said and sent them off site until the Queen had left the garden.

"Sorry about that Ma'am. They were checking the alarms."

"Yes, well there are no alarms in my Summer House, Officer."

The workmen looked pretty alarmed...

"No Ma'am, I've pointed them in the right direction."

US State visit

During the US State visit, all annual leave was cancelled. Preparations got underway to host George W. Bush and his entire cavalcade at the Palace. The advance party of Secret Service agents had been taken out of their boxes and wound up, and were carrying out all manner of recces. There were suddenly lots of people in suits with marine haircuts speaking into their sleeves trying to look important. On our Manor!

I was working with my good friend Ben one day when we were approached by two Special Agents. They looked like clones of each other. Dark pressed suits, cropped hair and Ray bans.

The first agent spoke. "Sir, ma'am, we're Secret Service agents." He flipped open his badge holder which was holding the largest badge I had ever seen.

"Wow!" said Ben, "There's nothing secret about that badge is there?"

"Excuse me sir?" said the Special Agent.

"Well, King Arthur could have used that as a shield," said Ben.

"I'm not following you sir," said the clone.

"You know, Excalibur? Knights of the round table?" Ben continued. The Special Agent just continued staring at Ben without cracking a smile.

"Never mind," said Ben, giving up on the history lesson. "How may we assist you today?"

"Thank you sir. We need to gain access to the Royal Moys."

"I think you mean The Royal Mews," said Ben while giving them directions.

"Thank you sir, ma'am," and off they marched stiffly down Buckingham Gate.

"I heard the new models came with built in humour sensors for working overseas," said Ben. "Must be a rogue batch."

Things were starting to get really cramped in our building while the Yanks were staying. SO19 snipers had taken over our gym and there were that many officers on security patrols that needed feeding, that our canteen was full of general duties coppers. When we came off post, we had nowhere to sit down, we couldn't use the gym and the queue for food was out the door.

The canteen staff were getting pissed off and everyone started bickering at each other. There was a quite clearly defined pecking order though. I mean, I wasn't going to tell the SO19 guy to move his feet, he had a bigger gun than me, so I picked on a shiny looking probationer that had been sitting on a comfy seat for an hour watching TV. "Come on mate, you're starting to grow roots there."

Then Mary our Nigerian canteen manager burst out of the kitchen with her tea towel over her shoulder shouting, "A' HAVE HAD ENOFF! ALL OF YOU, GET OUT!"

Mary was only about 5ft 2 inches tall and quite buxom, but not one to be underestimated. She was usually very mild mannered, but a few things would set her off such as ordering the "Met 999 all day breakfast" at lunchtime.

"But Mary, it says **all day**."

"A' know what it says but it is now lonch time. Choose something off de lonch menu."

"But I don't want anything of the lunch menu, I want a Met 999."

"Well a' can make you one, but you will haffto wait."

"Well how long?"

"A' do not know. Maybe **all day**!"

Mary continued clearing the canteen. "And you, take your feet off de table!" she said as she cracked her tea towel at the SO19 guy. She got him right on the tip of his ear making him flinch and spill his coffee all over his trigger finger. She was a crack shot, Mary. Everyone jumped out of their seats. Even with a semi-automatic weapon, it was a fool who would take on Mary's tea towel. Respect the pecking order.

Just as everyone was heading for the door, a down draft slammed it shut as 'Marine One' hovered over the garden as it came in to land. We were used to helicopters landing in the garden but this was a bit of a beast. We all watched as it touched down and ten US Marines jumped out and stood to attention either side of the aircraft doors. George Dubya Bush then stepped out of the helicopter and was led up to the house.

Our Marines then marched themselves across the lawn towards our building. "Oh my god, we're under attack!" Ben shouted. "They're heading straight for us."

"Well, a' am not feeding them too!" said Mary and folded her arms with her tea towel draped over in a semi-draw position. They came out of the garden, up the police building stairs and marched in time across the front of our canteen while we all stared open mouthed. "Heft, right, heft, right, heft, right, heft…" Absolutely priceless. We all just looked around at each other and fell about laughing.

'Jar Head' meets Buckingham Palace. How surreal. The balance had finally been restored. SO14 and SO19 officers, our beat bobbies and the canteen staff were all one happy Met Police family again.

The following day, I was working on the corridor outside one of the private apartments when George Dubya Bush came along the corridor.

Oh great, what exactly do I refer to him as, Sir? Mr President? George?

"Good morning officer. What a great day!" he said.

"Yes Sir, Mr George President, it's a lovely day."

Oh good grief…

I headed out to the garden about 8.45am. Jim, the Queen's Pipe Major, was about to start playing the bagpipes on the terrace in front of the Queen's apartment. This occurs religiously each morning at 9.00am.

Just as he started playing, we were interrupted by a loud banging on the other side of garden gate. I opened the wicket gate to see a Rayban wearing clone staring back at me. He flashed me his badge which was frankly too large to be seen through the wicket.

"That's lovely, how can I help you?" I asked.

"Cadillac One needs to gain access to the Western Terrace ma'am," said the clone.

"Western Terrace? That sounds like a cowboy film. Do you mean The West Terrace?"

"Yes sir, ma'am!"

"Excuse me? Did you just say 'Yes sir, ma'am?'"

"No sir. Yes. I mean no ma'am"

"Oh my god."

"We are Secret Service ma'am, we need to do a dry run for the President's cavalcade tomorrow."

"And which President would that be sir?" I asked.

"The President of the United States of America ma'am."

"Well I'm awfully sorry sir, but the Queen's piper is on the terrace and we can't allow any vehicles through the gate at this time. It's totally against protocol," and I smiled and shut the wicket gate.

Two minutes later, I got a phone call from our Operations guy Alec. "Cat, stop playing with the Secret Service agent that's a good girl." So I begrudgingly had to let them in.

Later that day I was working out the front with Sue, one of the other female officers. We received a two-minute warning that the Queen and the Duke were on their way back from Westminster. One minute later a Secret Service car pulled up outside the entrance within the sterile area. Two clones jumped out looking all important with their ear pieces in and started talking into their sleeves. They were blocking the entrance to the Palace.

Sue went over to the car and said, "Oy, mate, you can't park that there!"

"Excuse me ma'am? But we're Secret..."

"Yeah we know how secret you are, but you can't park there!"

"But ma'am, we're checking our radio frequencies."

"I think you'll be able to tune into whichever station you want round 'ere mate. Try Capital Radio! Now move your bloomin' car, we've got Royals coming in!" and she waved them on. With that, two of George Bush's finest Secret Service Agents jumped in their car sheepishly and sped up Constitution Hill. The Secret Service were the best toys we'd been given to play with in ages.

It was the official opening of the State visit and the world's media were set up at the front of the Palace. I was working with my mate Pete. It was our job to stand either side of garden gate and salute the President as he drove out. We received a radio message to say that President George W. Bush was "on the move" from "Western Terrace" towards Garden Gate in Cadillac One. We waited till the car came into sight at the corner

of the West Terrace and we opened up the heavy double doors. I have to admit to being a little taken aback as we locked them in place. A million flashes went off simultaneously. It was blinding. Every country with a flag had their cameras pointed at those gates. Here was the most powerful man in the world being hosted by the Queen of England on a State Visit.

The Mall looked amazing with the Stars and Stripes and Union Flags as far as the eye could see. A sudden feeling of pride washed over me as the first gun went off. Nobody does pomp like the Brits and we were welcoming the Americans with a forty-gun salute.

Pete and I stood to attention either side of the gates and as Cadillac One drew level we both gave the most military precision salutes we could muster. Perfect. Sky News chose to put that clip in their loop so we could be berated by our colleagues in the canteen over and over and over again.

One week later Elvis left the building and took all his little puppets with him. The Palace could finally get back to its normal organized chaos.

The Palace Christmas Ball

That year my partner Alex and I received an invite to the Queen and Duke of Edinburgh's Christmas Ball held at Buckingham Palace. It was a black tie dinner so we opted for matching tuxedos. I wore a burgundy silk waist coat with matching cravat and Alex opted for the silver silk waist coat and cravat. We looked the business.

As the Christmas ball got nearer, I asked what kind of reception we would receive wearing tuxedos, as opposed to cocktail dresses. Whenever a female guest at a Garden Party or reception contacted the palace to ask if it was acceptable to wear trousers, the stock answer from the palace was always, "Well, madam, the Queen will not be wearing trousers."

Personally, I doubt the Queen was overly concerned about her guest's choice of attire. I was told by one member of the household that considering we had been invited by 'Her Majesty' the least we could do was dress appropriately.

"What exactly is appropriately?" I asked.

"For ladies, black tie means a formal dress or a cocktail dress," she replied.

"Well I don't own either, nor would I be seen dead in one," I answered.

"Well, the Queen won't like it," she said.

There was that phrase again, "The Queen won't like it." I had a sneaky suspicion that she wasn't as close to the Queen as that statement immediately implied. She was part of the "Queen won't like it" Brigade.

These tended to be the middle ranking members of the household who felt they had something to prove. They were the ones who would refuse to show their passes on their way in to the palace, insisting you should know who they are. Some of them were also distinguished members of the "Don't you know who I am?" Brigade. We never had that problem with senior members of the house. They always showed their passes and were always very polite.

Our cab dropped us off at the Grand Entrance and one of the Paige's lead us into Marble Hall. The choir was singing Christmas carols in the corner of the hall next to an enormous Norfolk pine Christmas tree. It was very festive. We headed up the grand staircase which was lined

with Paige's in red tunics, one on each step. When we reached the top of the stairs, we were both handed a sugar rimmed flute of champagne. What a great start.

Almost all of the State rooms were being used for the function, all with different themes. The picture gallery was a winter wonderland, one of the drawing rooms had been turned into a nightclub which was playing Kylie Minogue's 'Can't get you out of my head.' It seemed almost surreal. There was a Rembrandt that I had always stopped to look at on our patrols around the palace. It was a bargain at seven million pounds and there were no ropes or barriers stopping anyone walking right up and touching it. It just seemed wrong to allow people to stand so near to a masterpiece like this while they had a lit cigar in one hand and a glass of red wine in the other. I wasn't so sure that the Queen would like it.

As we walked back through the East gallery, I spotted the Master of the Household walking towards us with the Queen's Private Secretary.

The moment of truth...

Peer pressure is a very powerful thing. I almost turned tail and pulled Alex in the other direction but I stood my ground and he caught my eye, smiled and said, "Very smart ladies." I could finally relax. If the Master of the House didn't have a problem with what we were wearing, however unorthodox, I'm sure the Queen wouldn't mind.

Alex and I made our way towards the ballroom where most of the other guests were seated and began looking for our table. I spotted the "Queen won't like it" Brigade sitting about two tables over. The air of superiority was staggering. I could feel the judgement as we walked past but I didn't care. I pointed them out to Alex and we gave them a little smile and a wave and headed off to our table with disapproving huffs and tuts coming from behind us.

After the dessert course, we were all chatting and trying to empty our bottomless glasses, when there was a shuffling of chairs at the far end of the room and everyone started to stand up and form an orderly line on either side of the walkway. I could just make out Prince Philip walking through the crowd. It was customary for the whole family to walk through after the meal and chat to the staff. I had no intention of getting close enough for the Duke to pass comment on my choice of dress.

The Duke certainly wasn't backwards in coming forwards if he disapproved of something. Alex and I stood about three back from the front. As the Duke drew level with where we were standing, there was a bit of pushing and shoving from behind us and we were forced further back. We had been ousted by the Brigade who were now standing to attention waiting their turn to curtsey.

They probably met every Wednesday night to practice. They most likely knew more about Royal protocol than the Queen and the Duke. The Queen Mum used to call it red carpet fever, when members of the household become more Royal than the Royals. You could see it happening to some of the Close Protection officers too. Some would forget that they were police officers and in an effort to fit in they would start wearing tweeds and plus fours. Most of Royalty Protection's budget went on the Close Protection's clothing allowance and fleet of racing green Range Rovers.

I watched as the Duke got nearer to the Brigade and in his ever so tactful manner, he took one look at the Brigade leader while she was mid curtsey and said, "Oh god, not you again," and completely bypassed them and went onto the next guest.

Fanbloodytastic!

I laughed all the way back to my seat. You can smell a "yes" person a mile away and when you're surrounded by them daily, it must be nauseating.

The Palace Ball was a fantastic start to the festive season. Alex and I saw in the New Year with friends and I remember thinking that 2005 was going to be my year.

Chinks In The Armour

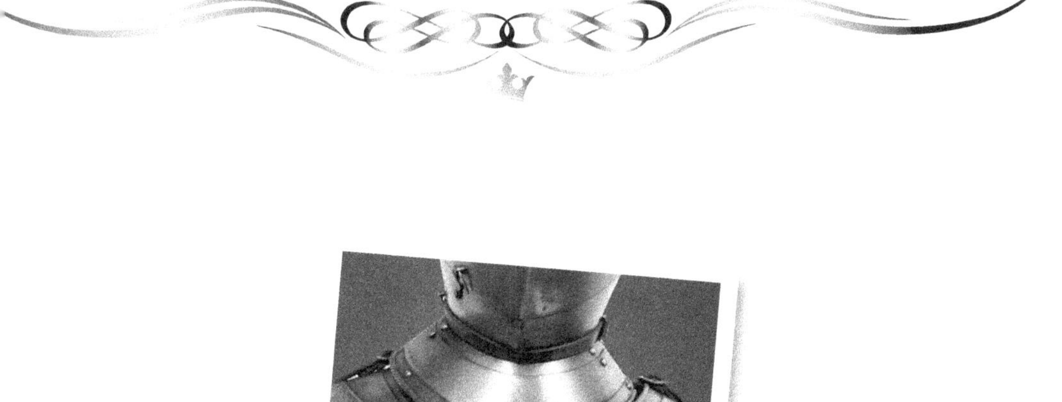

Chapter 8

Chinks In The Armour

"Vulnerability is not weakness. It is our most accurate measure of courage."

Brene Brown

I was wrong. The first six months of 2005 were completely shit and they were about to get worse. My duties for the 7th July were changed last minute. Prince Charles was hosting a function for old vintage car owners so I was required to work on the search team at St James Palace for a 9.30am start. It was just another day at the office, or so I thought.

I got on the Victoria line at Highbury and Islington station at about 8.45am. I intended on getting off at Green Park but when the train arrived at Kings Cross, there was an announcement stating that there had been an incident at the station and the train was being evacuated. I didn't want to be late so I headed for the Piccadilly line. When I got to the top of the escalators I was pushed back by a tide of people coming up. There was a young copper in front of me so I asked him what was going on.

"Not sure," he said. "Some incident on the Piccadilly line."

I tried to call work but I couldn't get a signal. Since I was wearing my

police blue search kit, I decided to head down to the Piccadilly line to see if I could help.

It's a funny word, help. It implies being able to assist, give relief, comfort. As I stood there amidst the chaos on that Piccadilly line platform, I realised I was too poorly equipped to do any of those things. To steal a quote from Robbie Burns, "Man's inhumanity to man, makes countless thousands mourn." No amount of training could prepare me for the sheer devastation that one human being could willingly inflict on another with a backpack full of homemade explosive. I had never felt so helpless in my entire life.

I don't know what to do...

As a human being, our natural instinct is to help those in need and as a police officer, it's our job to preserve life. It goes against every moral fibre of our entire being to step over someone that you know you can do absolutely nothing for.

Please forgive me...

I have no idea how long I was down there. Just before I headed back up, I saw the young copper that I'd spoken to earlier. He was crying and had a mate either side of him helping him toward the escalators.

Bless him...

He looked brand new. Straight out of the box. Broken already. I felt bad that someone so young had to witness such carnage. Maybe he'd always dreamt of being a police officer. Maybe he joined wanting to help people, protect people. What then, when there is nothing you can do to help? What then? Looking back, maybe it was easier for me to see the chinks in his armour and feel concern for him rather than to have to notice the chinks in mine.

Don't you dare fall apart...

When I reached the concourse, it felt like everything was going on around me, as though I wasn't actually there. I felt like I was just an observer. I don't remember making a conscious decision to leave Kings Cross that day. All I recall is pushing through an outer cordon that a young P.C. was standing on and walking home in a daze.

Fifty-five people lost their lives that morning while making their way into work on that sunny day in July.

"Those who can make you believe absurdities can make you commit atrocities."

Voltaire

How do you go home and put the kettle on, watch Coronation Street and pretend that everything's the same as it was yesterday? I wasn't sure anything would ever be the same again. When I woke the next day, the world felt different somehow. Kind of grey and colourless. I felt numb.

A couple of weeks later, Occupational Health sent me a leaflet asking me if I needed counselling for trauma. It went straight in the shredder.

Why the hell would I need that?

All I needed was to get away for a while. Away from London.

Balmoral Castle

So this is where my story started, in the Forest of Death and Blood contemplating what a crap year 2005 had been. Running away to Balmoral was easy. A lot easier than dealing with the fallout of the 7/7 bombings. A lot easier than dealing with the fact that my relationship with Alex had irreparably broken down and for the first time in my life I was living alone.

The last year of our relationship had been awful. We were both desperately unhappy. I had fallen in love with Australia and planned on emigrating way before Alex and I even met. She knew that but hoped I would change my mind. She had the next five years of her career mapped out in the Met. We wanted completely different things. I felt trapped and I began resenting her so I would create arguments over the smallest thing. The biggest hurdle we encountered though, was my emotional stuntedness. Whenever there was a problem that required a mature discussion my "go to" phrase was generally, "Well, you know where the door is."

I really need to work on that…

When you keep pushing someone away, eventually they're too far away to come back. So, having heard it one too many times, Alex finally took my advice and walked through the door and out of my life.

Where the hell are you going?!

Balmoral had been a welcome distraction, but now I was sitting at Aberdeen airport waiting for my flight back to London and I didn't want to leave.

As we broke through the clouds, I looked across the city that had been home for eleven years. I had always been excited to arrive back in

London, but not today. It seemed sullied somehow. It had lost a lot of its colour. It didn't feel like home anymore. I called Lynda up and we went out for a drink. We got talking about my previous two relationships, which had slightly overlapped, and she gave it to me straight.

"Cath, you'd rather be in a co-dependent relationship that made you miserable than be on your own."

Who asked you?

I had always thought of myself as self-reliant and fiercely independent, but she was absolutely right. In the whole of my adult life, I had never really been single. I didn't know how to be single. I'd never come home to an empty house before. I had jumped from one relationship to another without ever stopping to deal with any of the emotional fallout. I realised to my horror, that my self-worth had been based on my relationships.

I feel sick…

The pain and discomfort that I was experiencing wasn't due to the break up. It was due to my lack of self-worth. How could I have a healthy relationship with someone else if I didn't know how have one with myself?

How very Oprah…

So, where was I to find this elusive self-worth then? I decided to go looking for it at the bottom of a pint glass in Soho, where I bumped into an old friend. To cut a long story short, I got into a rebound and almost destroyed a good friendship. I should have been wearing a warning sign.

Rebound-Keep Clear!

I had become one of those people I despised, clinging on desperately to a dying relationship. When that didn't work, I grabbed hold of the nearest person like they were the last life jacket on a sinking ship and almost dragged them under too.

How disgusting!

I was trying desperately to fill an emotional void. It was as though all my break ups had come back to haunt me in one massive reject-fest.

Perfect Imperfection

My Imperfections I have tried to Hide,
Behind this Mask, dwells a shame Inside.
Self-doubt and Fear torment me each day,
Haunted by the Love I keep pushing away.

To love Myself is my greatest Test,
For only then can I give my Best.
I have made mistakes, God only Knows,
For Those I love, I hurt the Most.

I am Sorry beyond words, that I hurt you my Friend,
My Soul I would sell, if your Heart it would mend.
A Friendship lost, is my greatest Regret,
For although I am Not, my love for you is Perfect.

The Pain Train

As my friend George says, "You'll never avoid pain, you'll just delay it." Well, my pain train had been delayed for about thirty years, not unlike

British Rail, but it was now careering full speed towards me and I was tied firmly to the tracks! I would have given Lisa a call but we weren't on speaking terms either. I think she found out it was me that pulled the Abba tapes apart. I had successfully pushed everyone that I cared for away.

Don't slam the door on the way out!

This meant I could sit in my flat alone with a bottle of Shiraz, feeling sorry for myself, and fire off drunken text messages to all my exes.

Don't underestimate how good it can make you feel, sitting there blaming the world for all your problems. I felt fabulously superior and self-righteous because of course none of it was my fault. It was everyone else. It took a couple more bottles of Shiraz, but the penny finally dropped and I realised that actually, I was the common denominator.

This is awkward…

I lacked all the skills required to hold down a personal relationship. I'd never learned how to. I had been awarded the eminent title of Ice Queen by previous partners, pleural. Lacking in emotion; stoic to the point of martyrdom.

Even my seven-year-old nephew, Dylan could see right through me.

"Aunty Cath. Why didn't you cry when you said goodbye to Granddad?"

"No reason mate."

"I know why. It's because you don't know how to express your emotions."

Whatever...

It's not easy keeping up with such a hard fought reputation. I had to bottle up every negative emotion I'd ever had for thirty years. Now I felt like a pressure cooker about to go off. On the odd occasion, when I felt some kind of emotion trying to seep through the cracks, I would head to my local pub, The Canonbury Tavern in Islington. The Canonbury was full of arty types so I could sit in the corner reading the Islington Gazette, nursing a large glass of Shiraz or three without being judged too harshly.

I woke up one Sunday morning and much to my disgust, I was actually starting to feel something. An emotion.

This is not good...

It needed to be suppressed and the pub wasn't open. I jumped in the car and headed to Sainsburys to get a bottle of Shiraz and some cheese, as though the cheese added a little finesse to buying a bottle of wine at 11.00am. When I got to the cheese aisle, they were all out of my favourite Castillo blue cheese.

And that's when it happened.

The shame of all shames…

I started crying uncontrollably. The pressure cooker had finally blown right there in the cheese aisle.

I abandoned my trolley and headed for the sanctuary of my VW Golf.

What is happening?

I abhorred any show of public emotion from anyone. It made me cringe.

The humiliation…

I cried for an hour.

I cried for my mum who never got to live a full life and see her kids grow up.

I cried for my dad who lost his wife.

I cried for my brothers and my sister who lost their mum.

I cried for the children whose parents never came home on the 7th July.

I may even have cried for all the ants I'd stepped on.

Finally, I cried for the five-year-old who was still angry with God.

When I had just about run out of tissues, the Sainsbury's security guard knocked on my window and asked if I was alright.

"I'm ok mate, they just ran out of blue cheese."

Know When to Ask For Help

This had gone way past the point of Shiraz. I needed real help. It meant I would finally have to take a good long look at myself, which I had successfully managed to avoid doing my entire life. No-one likes to appear vulnerable, least of all police officers. Take it from me, after all I was hiding behind a tonne of kevlar, 80 rounds of ammunition, an MP5 and a Glock. If that's not armouring up, what is? We hide behind the uniform projecting an image of strength and fearlessness, but in truth, we're just as vulnerable as everyone else. We just hate admitting it. We don't ask for help when we need it for fear of being seen as "not up to the job." We wear masks so people can't see the real us. We self-medicate.

Unfortunately, that means that the cases of suicide amongst police officers appears to be on the rise due to issues like PTSD. It is a sad statistic that police officers are five times more likely to die at their own hands than by any other means. Ultimately, it is our job to look after our own mental health. I remember a call coming in for an attempted suicide one night shift. When we arrived on scene, the guy was standing on the top of a 50 meter tower. Before anyone could do anything, he fell from the top. I was standing next to the dog handler. We both turned our backs and looked away as he came down. I took some small comfort from that. Neither of us wanted to witness it. The sound was bad enough. It was our job to pick up the pieces, but we did not have to have that image replay itself time and again. Call it self-preservation.

Lay Down Your Armour

The best police officers I have ever worked with have been able to lay down their armour and be themselves, authentic, understanding, filled with empathy. It was time for me to lay mine down. Making the appointment to see a therapist was the hardest phone call I ever made. At least this time I was going of my own volition and not under a legal order which made a change. I went to a few sessions, but I still wasn't quite ready to open up and accept full responsibility for the way my life was turning out. I still had some blame left in me and I was starting to enjoy the self-indulgent pleasure of sitting in the *victim* chair moaning about how bad my life was. It was a good old £30 an hour whinge-fest. My counsellor hardly said a word in any of the sessions. She would just occasionally nod and say, "And how did that make you feel?"

She recommended a group session to work with my "inner child." I'd never heard of it but I thought I'd give it a go. While we waited for the facilitator, I sat silently on my bean bag judging everyone else in the room.

Let he who is not seated on a bean bag throw the first stone.

As the session began, I soon realised it was more of a competition to see who had the most wounded inner child. The lady sitting opposite whose dad had picked her up late from school once started, "My inner child is lost and alone. She cries but no-one hears her. I hold her and whisper everything will be alright."

Is she for real?

I looked around the room hoping to make eye contact with someone. Surely I wasn't the only one thinking her inner child needed a slap.

Toughen up Princess!

"Thank you for sharing Clarice," said the facilitator. "Anyone else?"

"Yes," said a lady wearing a papoose, whose father made her go to bed

without a story when she was ten. "My inner child has no arms and legs. I pick her up, and rock her till she falls asleep."

For the love of Tiny Tim… Someone please say something!

I pictured her wheeling her inner child off a cliff.

"Thank you for sharing Petra. Would anybody else like to share?" She looked at me.

Ooh, don't open that box back up.

I was too ashamed to admit that my inner child was a complete psychopath who would probably set light to all the bean bags while we were still sitting on them.

Nope. Not letting her back out.

That box was to remain firmly under lock and key. There was no way I was going to embrace my inner child and I'm fairly certain she wouldn't let me anywhere near her.

At the end of the session, the facilitator and I decided that group therapy wasn't going to work for me. I made that sound like a joint decision, didn't I? It wasn't. She felt that I wasn't ready to engage in a group setting and added that my facial expressions when people were sharing, put them off fully opening up. I was a negative influence on the group.

Are you breaking up with me?

Unbelievable. Dumped by my own counsellor. To be honest, it was a relief. I'm just not a beanbag kind of girl. I wished Clarice and Petra all the best sorting their daddy issues out and jumped on the No 73 bus to Islington Green.

Victim

I don't want to hear words of comfort, or solutions to my woes,
Don't tell me thing will get better, it's just the way it goes,
That the wind will change direction and my problems will
disappear.
For who am I without them, I've grown accustomed to this fear.

I just want you to acknowledge, you've never been through worse,
Whatever hardship you've faced, it can't compare to this curse.
When I'm drowning in self-pity you'll hear me cry, "Why me?"
But now it's strangely comforting wallowing in this misery.

So don't tell me to keep smiling, you'll never understand,
Because only I could have been dealt such an awful hand!
And I don't want to keep my chin up, I'm happy head turned
down,
Nor hear witty remarks, how it takes less muscles to smile than
frown.

I've nothing to be grateful for, my life is in a mess,
None of it's my fault; I point the finger of blame at everyone else!
So I turn my cheek and absolve myself from any responsibility,
And enjoy the fact that I can cry, "Poor me, Poor me, Poor me!"

The London Kabbalah Centre

Dredging up the most painful parts of someone's life and putting them under a microscope was never going to work for me. It wasn't my psyche that needed fixing, it was my spirit. When I got off the bus, I headed

to my local bookstore and went straight to the body, mind and spirit section looking for answers. My rucksack which I carried everywhere like a security blanket, knocked a book off the shelf. I picked it up off the floor and noticed it was a book by Yehuda Berg, "The Power of the Kabbalah." I had no idea what the Kabbalah was but it made promises to answer some soul searching questions so I bought it. What did I have to lose? I read it cover to cover in about two hours.

It all made perfect sense to me but left me with more questions. I headed over to the Kabbalah Centre in central London. I bought five more books and enrolled on a course called The Power of the Kabbalah. My Instructor Marcus Weston was extremely knowledgeable and I never once saw him stuck for an answer even on the most confronting questions asked by the students. That course was the most life changing course I have ever been on. What I loved the most about the Centre though was that it was such a melting pot of different races, creeds and religions. There were Muslims, Christians, Hindis and Jews, all under the same roof.

That's where I met my good friend Dean. Dean was my little godsend. Just when I needed a friend, there he was. He would rock up to the classes late every week, rushing in throwing apologies around while un-scarfing himself and finding a seat. His tardiness amused me. To be honest, I'm surprised he managed to get to the Centre at all. He was extremely busy running his modelling agency in Islington and he was constantly talent scouting. Dean used to be quite the party animal in his time, but all that changed after one particularly raucous New Year's Eve party. The host tapped him on the shoulder and told him his cab had arrived. Dean hadn't called a cab. He hasn't touched a drop since. Now he is a much sought after speaker at AA and NA meetings all over London. I held a lot of admiration for him and whenever we hung out, he showed me there was a lot more to life than just the pub. Who knew?

He talked me into cycling from London to Paris for 'Success for Kids', a non-profit organisation that aims to empower at-risk children and teens around the world. Dean hadn't ridden a bike for years, so if he was up for it, so was I. I dusted off my Rock-hopper and Dean borrowed a friend's mountain bike. There were about fifty of us that set off to France that day. Three days later we finally reached the outskirts of Paris. Dean was really struggling those last few miles. I asked him what gear he was in. "Gears? What gears darling?" he replied. I laughed so hard I almost fell off my bike. Dean had literally ridden the whole way without changing gears once. He should have been given a medal. But that was typical of Dean. He never complained once, he just kept plugging away for a solid 300 kilometers of undulating terrain in 5th gear. That's determination.

Everybody at the Centre had a story, a reason for finding their way to the door of that building in Stafford Place. One thing we had in common, we all wanted answers to some long held questions. I made a lot of good friends there, people who I could bounce all these new ideas off and keep me in check. The most profound yet simplest concept that I took away from the Centre was that I was responsible for everything in my life.

> *"If it's never our fault, we can't take responsibility for it. If we can't take responsibility for it, we'll always be its victim."*

Richard Bach

Cause and effect. Good and bad, if it was in my movie then it was there for a reason and I had the power to deal with it or change it. I was not a victim of circumstance. It meant taking full responsibility for everything. No more blame. Blaming makes you a victim. Being a victim makes you powerless. I came away from the Centre with some very valuable tools. I still had a lot of unanswered questions though, going right back to 1974. The first one was, "If God exists, why did he let fifty-five people get blown up on the 7th July?"

It all boils down to free will.

If love is the supreme ethic, then you cannot have love without intrinsically weaving into it free will. If God stopped each trigger from being pressed, then mankind would be like machines with no will of our own. For God to violate our free will, he is violating that which is a necessary component for love to be expressed.

I see...

I suppose I understood that on an intellectual level, but it took longer for me to 'get it' spiritually. The more I thought about it, the more I began to see a pattern behind the chaos. A bigger picture. In the midst of all the pain and suffering, there was also so much love. Perfect strangers were stopping to help bandage up the injured. Commuters were comforting crying relatives. First responders were running down into the depths of the Piccadilly line with no thought for their own safety. Buses and taxi drivers were ferrying the injured to hospital. It is in these moments of darkness and despair that our true nature shines through. It reminds us who we are and what we are truly capable of. It was no coincidence that I was on a later train that day at Kings Cross. I was exactly where I was supposed to be.

I replayed it over and over in my mind until I finally joined the dots.

*We are **all** connected…*

Every spiritual teaching tells us that, but I never really understood it till then.

There is no such thing as Us and Them. There is only Us.

So after thirty years, I finally had an answer.

Why does God let awful things happen? He doesn't. **We do**.

- If you ignore your emotions, they will eventually gang up on you and humiliate you in public. Find a way to let them go, talk to a friend, learn to meditate or even e-mail your rants to yourself.

- Vulnerability is not weakness; it is our most accurate measure of courage.

- Take full responsibility, for *everything*. Accept it like you chose it.

- No more blame. Blaming makes you a victim. Be the cause, not the effect.

Chapter 9

The Gift Of Relationships

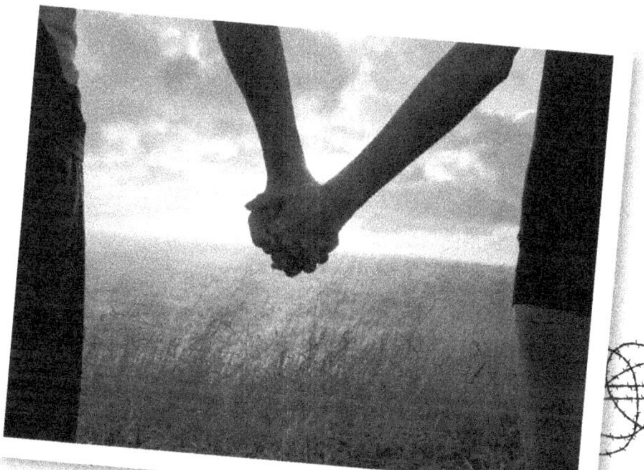

Chapter 9

The Gift Of Relationships

"Your task is not to seek for love, but merely to seek and find all the barriers within yourself that you have built against it."

Rumi

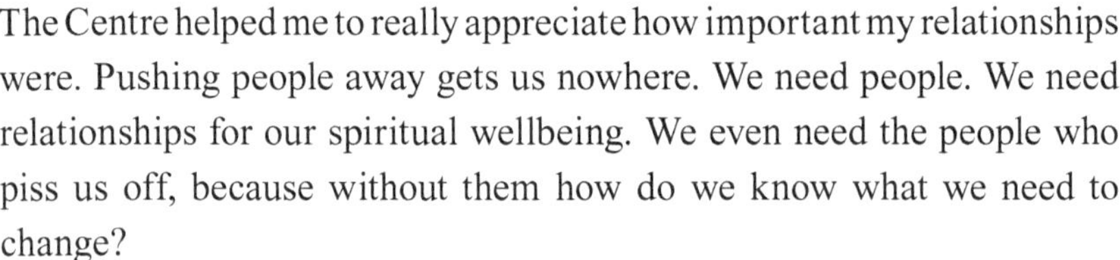

The Centre helped me to really appreciate how important my relationships were. Pushing people away gets us nowhere. We need people. We need relationships for our spiritual wellbeing. We even need the people who piss us off, because without them how do we know what we need to change?

My relationships were in dire need of fixing, so I turned to my coach and mentor, Tony Robbins. I don't mean I went to one of his five day seminars. I just bought myself a DVD boxset which I could watch in the relative safety and judgement free environment of my own front room.

According to Tony Robbins, people are motivated by the desire to meet six psychological needs. If we can't find a positive way to fulfil these needs, we will find a negative way.

Certainty – We want to avoid pain and feel that we are safe, secure. We like our little comfort zone, our safety net. Have you ever just clung on

desperately to a dying relationship? It's easy. Just hang on in there and when your partner tells you they're leaving, just hide their car keys and lock all the doors. Simple.

Uncertainty/variety – We need to experience a range of physical and emotional sensations. You can travel and immerse yourself in a completely different culture. You can start a new career or new relationship. Alternatively, you can jump from one relationship/crisis to another, tell your boss they're an arsehole, get sacked and go on an alcohol fuelled bender. Same result.

Significance – We all want to feel like we matter, that we have purpose, a sense of identity. We may excel at school or become high achievers, pillars of the community. Or you could steal a forklift truck and go on a low speed chase shouting, "You'll never take me alive!" and then when they do take you alive, collapse in a heap and pretend you're dead. Failing spectacularly is a great way to feel significant. Why work hard to achieve results when you can achieve the same level of significance by complete and utter failure? I swear by it.

Connection – We are hard wired for connection and love. We need to form bonds with other human beings. We need to belong. We can form meaningful relationships and friendships with our families, our partners and even our co-workers. And now with the advance of social media, people we've never even met can form scary imaginary relationships with us, until one day we come home and find them hiding in the back garden with a blindfold and some duct tape. To be honest, I'd probably be glad of the company.

Harvard carried out a study over 75 years, and the results found that what makes us the happiest is our relationships and feeling connected. In our most intimate relationships, if we don't feel we can rely on that person or we feel we are disconnected it affects physical health more so than the fallout from divorce.

Growth and Contribution – We need to grow; if we aren't growing, we die. We want to become more than we are so we have more to contribute and give back to our community, to the planet. We want to leave something of worth. The only way to feel truly fulfilled is to contribute.

The Kabbalah Centre talk about a concept called 'Bread of Shame', which explains that awful empty feeling we get when we are given something we feel we haven't earned. From a spiritual point of view, no-one really wants a free ride. We don't want something for nothing. That is why we always appreciate things more when we have to work harder for them. It also explains why generosity can breed resentment. Have you ever been around someone who never lets you pay for anything? It may seem nice at first, but after a while, it starts to feel uncomfortable. We all want the opportunity to share.

The primary purpose of relationships is to share, to magnify the human experience. Relationships are also where our expectations show up the most.

Great Expectations

"Expectation is the root of all heartache."

William Shakespeare

We all want our needs fulfilled so we enter relationships with a list of expectations. I want him to be emotionally available. I want her to be independent. I want him to be more romantic. I want her to not be a psychopath. Blah blah blah…

When they don't live up to the illusion we have built up in our head of the perfect partner, we begin to judge them for not living up to our expectations. We start to see them as flawed because they aren't fulfilling a need in us. But if the need is in us, who is lacking? We are.

It is not our partner's job to fix us or fill some emotional void left over from childhood. We expect our partners to be everything to us, to love us unconditionally, to always be there for us. It's all me, me, me.

Ironically, our expectations can illicit exactly those responses in the other person that we are trying to avoid. We can bring out the best and worst in people simply by communicating our expectation, almost like a self-fulfilling prophecy.

"I bet he hasn't put the bins out."

"I bet she starts nagging as soon as she comes in."

As Marianne Williamson said, we create what we defend against. When we lose our temper in relationships, it is generally due to an unfulfilled expectation. Maybe we would all be happier if we appreciated more and expected less. In an ideal world, we would enter a relationship asking simply, "What can I give?" Unfortunately, we place conditions on our affection. I promise to love you if you love me. If you can stop loving someone so easily, was it ever love to begin with? I think the true test of unconditional love is to see how much you still love someone when you can't stand them.

"To love for the sake of being loved is human, but to love for the sake of loving is angelic."

Alphonse de Lamartine

---

vul|ner|ability

1. to be exposed to the possibility of being attacked or harmed, either physically or emotionally

---

Opening up is scary, but to truly connect with another human being, we need to get comfortable with being vulnerable. Letting someone see the real you, behind the mask, is always going to be a scary process because you risk being rejected. Telling someone you love them, not knowing if those feelings will be reciprocated is about as scary as it gets, but what is the alternative? Stay in our comfortable little risk free boxes? Never taking a chance and never truly connecting with anyone? Who wants to lead that kind of life?

"Vulnerability is the only true bridge to connection."

Brene Brown

I built impenetrable walls throughout my childhood and well into my teens and they probably served me well back then. I hid my emotions

extremely well. As a youngster, I learned that being vulnerable in a hostile world was going to get you mullered! As an adult, I realised that no-one can sustain a relationship with someone that can seemingly turn their emotions off in an instant. I'm still working on it. Writing this book is the scariest thing I have ever done, but it's part of my effort to embrace vulnerability. When you open up and show people the real you, it also gives them permission to do the same. You can't connect with someone through brick walls.

Embrace Singledom

I read somewhere that some relationships are brought to us to teach us how to let go gracefully with complete forgiveness for the other person.

How very grown up...

I can honestly say there has been absolutely nothing graceful about any of my break ups. There was not one shed of forgiveness being given. In fact, I had a copy of the Yellow Pages thrown at my head during one of them. What a golden opportunity to post obscure attention seeking status updates...

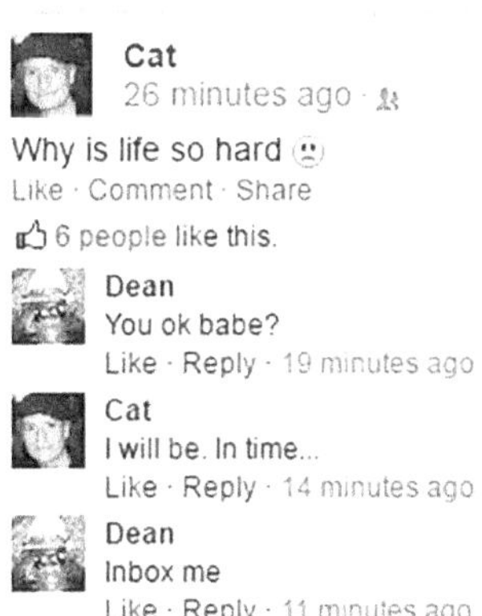

Why are we all so scared of being single? I know I certainly was. My self-worth deteriorated when I wasn't in a relationship so I made a conscious decision to stay single until I'd fixed myself. Staying single in London wasn't as easy as it sounds. I stopped going out and had to delete my Facebook account so I wasn't tempted to look up any of my exes.

Don't judge me, we've all done it.

Before Facebook you had to actually get in your car to stalk your ex. Now you don't even have to leave the house. Granted, it's probably not as satisfying as driving slowly past your ex's house at 2.00am, but you're less likely to get a restraining order served on you.

I believe the space in between relationships is where we truly learn how to accept and eventually love ourselves. If you don't love yourself, then you will inevitably enter a relationship looking to get that, rather than to give. You can't pour from an empty cup as they say. I think, knowing how to be alone and happy in your own company is a prerequisite for a successful relationship.

We don't need to be in a relationship to be validated. I was horrified whilst listening to the radio when a lady being interviewed was asked why she was still single. She replied, "If I knew, I'd do something about it," as though there was something wrong with her.

She was obviously painfully aware of the stigma attached to being a single female, whereas I was completely oblivious to it. I hadn't received the memo. I was feeling particularly upbeat on my way out of work one evening, when my Sergeant took umbrage to my cheerful disposition and decided to point out my sad and lonely status to the whole team. He stuck out his bottom lip and asked me, in a baby voice, "So, what are you going to do tonight Cat? Go home alone and veg on the couch?"

Brilliant. I'm Bridget Jones.

I found the remark so offensive, I just stared at his bottom lip for three seconds before replying.

How very dare you...

"Actually, I'm going to the gym, then out for a meal with friends."

It was a complete lie. I was absolutely going home to veg on the couch, but it was my choice.

How sad am I?

Being single has more stigma attached than being gay. Who knew?

I thought about his comment on the way home and it really pissed me off, which wasn't too difficult being as though I'd been angry since 1974. Did he think that not being in a relationship made me less of a person? The more I thought about it, I realised that actually, it was all about him. He had married his teen sweetheart and had never been single. He was petrified of being alone. People like that tend to project their fears onto other people and try and make you feel like there's something wrong with you.

I shrugged off his comment and had a delightful 'Bridget Jones' night in. Truth is, I started to enjoy my own company a bit too much and I have to say, I'm a pretty good best mate. I've never let me down yet. I am far from perfect, but I accept myself completely, warts and all. It may be a cliché, but ultimately, the most important relationship you will ever have, is with yourself.

The Gift

*You trespass uninvited in my dreams at night,
Taunting me constantly from my sleep, never a
moments respite. I reach out in the darkness,
but you're no longer there. Rather suffer an arrow
from an archer's bow, than know you're lying next to her...*

*I took your love for granted, so you walked out the
door. And on that day I saw your perfection and
became blind to all your flaws. Time has passed and eased
the pain, but the memory lingers on, I learned never to
idealise another soul, I held on for far too long...*

*The Gift you gave me was priceless, a true blessing in
disguise. I conquered my fear of being alone, and gained
my freedom as my prize. At the heart of every ending hides
the gate to your infinite desires... The Key, to let go of your
attachments with certainty that this too shall pass.*

*Don't narrow your choice of options, believing that they
were the One. Accept that this chapter is over, it's time
for you to move on. Pain is optional after a time, and
these things you should know, While you hold on
to the past, the future is waiting... Let go, Let go, Let go…*

---

for|give

1. stop feeling angry or resentful towards (someone) for an offence, flaw, or mistake.

The inability to forgive someone is the cause of many ruined friendships and relationships. Why do we find it so difficult? Forgiving someone doesn't mean you are letting them off the hook. If they betrayed you, you're never likely to trust them again. Trust is about the future; forgiveness is about the past. Forgiving is a way of releasing you from any hurt and anger you may still be feeling. You don't forgive someone for their sake, you forgive them for yours. Hanging on to resentments causes you to form a toxic attachment to that person.

I held a grudge against someone for over two years. I couldn't even hear her name mentioned without the anger building up in the pit of my stomach. My heart would race and I would literally feel sick. Meanwhile she was probably getting on with her life completely oblivious to the effect she was still having on me. The damage had been done by the original betrayal, but I was pouring fuel on the fire by holding onto that anger. It was only harming me, but I felt unable to let it go.

Deepak Chopra says to forgive someone you must defeat the three dragons: Judgement, Anger and Blame. If you are hanging onto a negative emotion, it is usually because you are gaining a secondary benefit for doing so.

Judgement has the secondary benefit of making you feel justified and morally superior, after all, she was obviously a disloyal, untrustworthy and immoral little bitch.

Isn't it ironic that we only judge people in areas where we are likely to feel the most shame? We don't judge people in those areas where we are self-assured and secure. So when we gossip and bitch, which we all love to do, it's like laying all our own insecurities out on the table.

Both the Kabbalah and Buddhism teaches that when you judge someone else, that person is just a mirror reflecting back to you all the negative traits that you need to work on yourself. That is a difficult concept for us to grasp, especially when someone irritates the hell out of us. Even our enemies can be our greatest teachers. It's very easy to remain spiritual and loving when you're surrounded by nice, easy going people. It's a lot harder when you're surrounded by complete idiots! (I have a long way to go…)

"We only recognise in others that which is in our self."

Law of Mirrors

Blame has the secondary benefit of putting the responsibility in someone else's lap. It also meant I didn't have to examine any wrongdoing on my part, because of course there wasn't any. It was completely her fault.

The only way to free yourself from blame, is to take responsibility for the situation. If your partner cheated on you, betrayed you, or left you suddenly, find a way to take some responsibility for the situation. There is no such thing as *suddenly*. There is always a seed that has been planted at some point in the past. As soon as you take responsibility for your part, however small, you stop being a victim and you can move forward.

Anger has the secondary benefit of justifying any vengeful feelings or hostile and aggressive behaviour, which made me feel less guilty about wishing she'd get hit by a bus.

Anger is easier to deal with than grief and sadness so it's a good 'go to' emotion. The Buddhists say, "Holding onto anger is like drinking poison and expecting the other person to get sick."

The Centre for Disease Control states that 85% of disease has an emotional element. It has long been thought that repressed emotions such as anger and resentment can manifest in diseases such as cancer and heart disease.

Oh dear...

I had thirty years of repressed emotion coursing through my veins like toxic waste. I was a prime candidate for a complete melt down the size of Chernobyl. What are we supposed to do with all that negative emotion? Putting a lid on it doesn't work, I tried that.

I truly believe the best way to deal with it is to learn to forgive everyone that you still harbour ill feeling towards, starting with ourselves. We are our own harshest critic. Forgiving someone is difficult, especially when that person isn't even sorry for what they have done. They may refuse to apologise, or at least acknowledge the hurt they have caused, but will their apology erase the hurt? Probably not, so why insist on one? Some people are emotionally incapable of apologising. They are unable to separate their actions from their character. If they did something bad, they must be bad people. Learn to accept the apology you never received.

Rabbi Harold Kushner said that if after two days, you still haven't forgiven someone for something, it becomes your responsibility. Two years was really pushing it. Was my friend actually a bitch? No, she wasn't. It was just easier for me to think of her that way, but you can detest someone's actions without detesting the person. At the end of the day, she was just trying to fulfil one of her own needs. Love, connection, significance, who knows. Her betrayal was actually nothing to do with me and everything to do with her.

Like Atticus said in To Kill a Mocking Bird, "You never really understand a person until you climb into his skin and move around in it." That actually sounds more like Silence of the Lambs, but I get what he's saying. Very often when we feel wronged, it rarely has anything to do with us. It boils down to the other person trying to fulfil their own needs. Once we take ourselves out of the equation, it's easier to let it go. We are all human, none of us are perfect and I would hate to get to the end of my life and know that there was someone out there who couldn't bring themselves to forgive me my mistakes. Worse than that though, would be to get to the end of my life and realise that I hadn't been able to forgive them theirs.

We learn a lot about trust and forgiveness through our immediate family, our children, our parents and siblings. Unfortunately, these are the people we tend to be the hardest on. Maybe we have higher expectations of them so we are more disappointed when they let us down. We bear grudges for years, but maybe we're missing the point. Some of our most important relationships are the ones that wind us up the most. The ones that truly test us. Brothers and sisters know exactly how to push each other's buttons. That's their job. Lisa and I have been pushing each other's buttons our whole lives.

Well she started it!

That's actually not true. I started it. I set the tempo of our relationship with my mini climbing expedition into Lisa's cot when she was six weeks old. I sank my teeth into her arm. Mum bit me back. I never did it again, at least not when mum was looking. I treated Lisa with the same contempt you would treat any stranger that you found hanging off your mother, the source of all your love and contentment.

Get off me mum!

Maybe I was always destined to be slightly high maintenance, who knows. Before mum got sick, we had all been living in Lisbon, Portugal for three years, that's where Lisa was born. I spoke fluent Portuguese which was fantastic because it meant I could terrorise everyone in more than one language. One weekend, we were visiting a village market in the hills in Sintra, when a gypsy couple mistook me for a Portuguese child. They kidnapped me and took me back to their caravan. True story.

They gave me back after half an hour. Seriously, what is that supposed to do to a kid's self-esteem?

When Lisa and I were at boarding school, I hardly said one word to her the whole time we were there. I didn't want anyone to see through my rock-hard façade. We had always shared a room and it took me a while to settle into sharing with girls I didn't even know. One night I couldn't sleep so I went to Lisa's dorm. She was fast asleep. I got such a lump in my throat seeing her there. I walked back to my dorm in tears because I felt so sad for her. She was too young to be there. One of the girls in my dorm heard me crying and she actually bit me! I never did it again.

Siblings have a habit of falling into the same patterns of behaviour that they have always shown each other. We may not be using the 'back of the arms squeezy pinch' method anymore, but we can use words like an arrow. Lisa and I have prodded each other constantly, because ultimately, we both want to know that there is someone out there who loves us unconditionally. I know, no matter what happens, Lisa will always be the first person I will call when I need someone.

Recently, when we hadn't spoken for a few months, she called me to ask if I would go with her to the breast clinic. Of course I dropped everything and went and when she was diagnosed with breast cancer, I cried myself to sleep every night for two weeks. It was a horrible feeling knowing there was nothing I could do to fix it. It was all out of my control. I had to concentrate on the things I could control, like looking after Dylan, or making carrot, kale and turmeric smoothies that tasted like vom!

I'm still working on that namby-pamby stuff and nonsense, so I found it easier to throw myself into something physical instead. I signed up for the Ride to Conquer Cancer and cycled 220km on a mountain bike and donated my backside to The Harry Perkins Institute for Cancer research. Next time I'll do a little training first.

I am extremely grateful that Lisa is now on the mend, but sometimes it takes something like this to happen for us to realise what is truly important. Each relationship is a gift and that person is only on loan to us. Whether they are a partner, a friend, brother, sister or parent. One day we will have to say goodbye. Nothing lasts forever. We should remind ourselves every day so we can truly appreciate all that they bring into our lives. Through our relationship, I have learned trust, forgiveness, unconditional love and a bit of mixed martial arts grappling.

Never take any relationship for granted.

**

My little sis...

- Expectation leads to disappointment. Appreciate more, expect less.

- Embrace Singledom. Become your own best friend.

- Vulnerability is the only true way to connect with another person.

- Our level of happiness is in direct proportion to the quality of our intimate relationships.

- Learn to forgive *everyone*, starting with yourself. None of us are perfect.

Gambling With Tomorrow

Chapter 10

Gambling With Tomorrow

"Twenty years from now, you will be more disappointed by the things that you didn't do than by the ones you did do, so throw off the bowlines, sail away from the safe harbor, catch the trade winds in your sails. Explore, dream, discover."

Mark Twain

Death The Great Leveller

No-one since time was invented has ever escaped death. Not Jesus, not Buddha, no Kings, no Queens. We are all equal in that respect. As the poet James Shirley wrote in the 16th Century:

Scepter and crown must tumble down and in the dust be equal made, With the poor crooked scythe and spade.

Of the seven billion people on the planet, approximately 56 million will die this year. That works out at about 150 thousand people a day. For some, death will be a long waited and welcome companion. For most, he will be an uninvited gate crasher.

In the Hindu culture, the bodies of the dead are washed by family members and taken to the banks of the Ganges to be cremated on funeral pyres. Death is a very public occasion. In Western countries, death is taboo. Dead bodies are hidden away and plied with makeup, hoping to make them look in death just as they were in life. We are shielded from the inevitability of our own mortality. We stick our heads in the sand and try not to think about it.

Buddhist monks regularly contemplate their own death in order to recognise how precious and short life is. By meditating on the inevitability of death, they hope to live a full and meaningful life and also prepare for the next.

At the Kabbalah Centre we completed an exercise where we imagined our own funeral. We had to ask ourselves:

- Who would be there?
- What they would say about us?
- How would we be remembered?

It was a very confronting but powerful exercise and it left me really appreciating each day as a gift. How can we truly appreciate the life we have been given if we never fully contemplate how easily it can be taken away? Anyone who has been given a life threatening diagnosis or had a near death experience will tell you, that is when they really started living and appreciating each moment.

Alan Watts, the great British philosopher said, "If you had a choice to delay death, you wouldn't delay it indefinitely." Knowing that one day, the clock will stop for us, gives us a sense of urgency to get things done and to live a purposeful life. As I get older, I feel that sense of urgency more acutely. I don't want to die with regrets.

Top Five Regrets of the Dying

Bonnie Ware nursed many dying patients over an eight year period and these were the five most common regrets of those nearing the end of their life:

1. I wish I'd had the courage to live a life true to myself, not the life others expected of me.

2. I wish I hadn't worked so hard.

3. I wish I'd had the courage to express my feelings.

4. I wish I had stayed in touch with my friends.

5. I wish that I had let myself be happier.

Personally, I have always had a problem keeping in touch with friends and family. I have just always expected that if someone wants to see me, they will call. That hasn't always worked out for me. Remember my politically incorrect mate Shazza that I mentioned in Chapter 5? She was a really good friend during my days in the Met, but we lost touch.

In September 2015, I was still sitting on the fence of crippling self-doubt, wondering whether to publish this book. I travelled to Melbourne to visit Darren Stephens, my publisher. That same weekend I found out that Sharon had been killed in a car accident while on holiday in Greece. I was devastated. She was too young and too full of life. I had plenty of opportunities to contact her on my travels, but life got in the way and now I'll never get that opportunity again. I signed up with Darren's company that weekend, because none of us know when our tomorrow is going to come.

So, Shazza, I'm sorry we never got to have that pint. Wherever you are, I hope you're still clearing the canteen of all the senior staff.

Guilt of Angels

The day your conscience told you what was right or wrong,
Was the day those chains of guilt began pulling you along,
Don't do this, you must do that or you won't enter Heaven,
The Fear of God instilled in us from the age of Seven.

And so it sets the scene for a lifetime of frustration,
Unfulfilled desires, Shattered dreams and Aspirations,
Torn between your longings and your family obligations,
You're caught up in a web of your parents' expectations.

You're through them but not from them, your life is yours alone,
Twenty years from now you'll wonder where the time has gone.
Too many lives are wasted due to this self- imposed restriction
Wracked with guilt and bound due to an Act or an Omission.

And there are those that seek to keep you in this place,
Pulling on your heartstrings, a sad look upon their face,
Don't listen when they cry, "Why have you done this to me?"
You cannot be held responsible for their victim mentality.

Guilt becomes a habitat and a familiar friend indeed,
Staying in your comfort zone, it's just the excuse you need.
It is such a heavy burden to carry through your life,
Dragging it round like luggage, wouldn't you rather travel light?

So Break those chains that bind you and then you'll be set free,
You've been a prisoner all your life, Guilt's your worst enemy,
Our time on Earth is fleeting, that's a fact that we all know,
So why wallow in things you cannot change, Simply Let them
Go...

Be Grateful for the Present

"If you are depressed, you are living in the past. If you are anxious you are living in the future. If you are at peace you are living in the present. "

Lao Tzu

Don't get caught up in the "I'll be happy when…" trap.

I'll be happy when I have the big house, the fast car or the perfect relationship. There is no such thing as a perfect relationship, and material things don't make us happy in the long run. What we really want is the feeling we get from having those things, so in the end, we aren't chasing the big house or the fast car. We are chasing a feeling, an emotion.

Some people think that having a large bank balance will make them happy, but just as many rich people commit suicide as poor. Being able to have everything they want at a moments' notice doesn't make them as happy as they thought it would. Maybe not getting everything you want is an indispensable part of happiness.

When we lack gratitude and appreciation for what we have, we complain and find fault. Complaining makes us unhappy and unfulfilled, so what do we do? We complain. It is a vicious cycle.

We cannot achieve true happiness by trying to fulfil our own selfish desires. We must help others fulfil their desires. The more we help

others, the more fulfilled and happy we feel. Most people wait to be happy before feeling grateful. They don't realise that happiness is actually the result of being grateful. If you can't be happy in the present moment, what makes you so sure you'll be happy in a future present moment? We're all waiting for the right time to be happy. Why not now?

Find Your Gift and Share it

"Be aware of the place where you are brought to tears… That is where your treasure is."

Paulo Coelho - The Alchemist

When I first read that line, I couldn't help but think of the cheese aisle in Sainsburys. Was my treasure really buried under the 'cheese of shame?' Maybe it was a metaphor for all the crap I had buried over the years and refused to deal with.

One side effect of my little meltdown was that I started to write. It was just a bit of poetry to start with. Nothing serious. I could stop if I wanted to. But things got out of hand and before I knew it, I was hanging around on street corners trying to score an ode or two. Maybe writing was my gift. Perhaps I had found a way to contribute by telling my story. I have always loved books. I read the complete library of Ladybird books before I left primary school. Reading was an escape.

Whatever it is that you want to do, don't let anyone try and talk you out of it. When I told people I was writing a book, someone asked, "Why would anyone want to read your book?"

I told him he was missing the point. I *wanted* to write it. Then I unfriended him on Facebook!

So mature...

Don't listen to the scaremongers and dream stealers who want to keep you in your safe little box, or those people that like to remind you not to get above yourself, with comments like, "Who do you think you are?" and "What makes you think you're good enough?" People like that generally don't make anything of their lives and they don't want you to either. Listen to your heart. Just ask yourself, what do I truly love to do? Our gifts may well be buried under our own personal struggles and hardship, because that is where we can contribute the most.

Being a police officer has fulfilled some of my needs, but it is a vocation, not a passion. The moments in the job where I have felt fulfilled have been the times when I know I have made a difference in someone else's life. There is no better feeling than helping someone else. It is also the best cure for depression. We can all wallow in self-pity every now and again but as soon as you stop thinking about yourself and put someone else first, it's impossible to stay miserable.

In this job, we tend to come into contact with people at their lowest ebb, but you should never judge someone by their worst moment. Some of the most fascinating conversations I have had have been in the lock-up. I have always been interested in what makes people tick. What decisions led them to that point in their life? I have spent countless hours listening to people talk about their relationship problems, drug and alcohol addictions, family dramas, domestics. I have gained some very valuable insights into what really drives people to do what they do. I enjoy it.

When I look back over the most important stages of my life, I have always had a mentor to help me through. Liz my social worker, John in the Royal Engineers, Lynda in the Met, my friend Dean, Marcus at the Kabbalah Centre and I mustn't forget Tony Robbins without whom I never would have gotten in the army or the police.

I realised that I had a wealth of experience behind me that I could use to help and mentor other people. So when I saw that Tony Robbins and Chloe Madanes had teamed up and were running a coaching programme, I signed up. I am now a certified Strategic Intervention coach, specialising in relationships issues.

Don't laugh...

Ironic I know, but if your relationship is falling apart would you rather speak to a twenty-five-year-old counsellor with a degree who married her high school sweetheart, or someone who has fallen at every hurdle, whose face is muddied, knees grazed and still made it across the line?

Exactly.

To quote Alan Watts again, "What would you do if money were no object?"

Forget the money. It is stupid to spend your whole life doing things you don't like, in order to go on doing things you don't like.

Why don't we all live the life we want to live? Fear of failure? Fear of criticism? Fear of rejection? Here's the thing, most of us won't be here in a hundred years, so what does it matter anyway?

> *"The wealthiest place is the cemetery, there lies companies that were never started, masterpieces that were never painted... Don't go to the grave with your treasure still inside you."*
>
> Myles Munroe

Set Goals and Take Action

"The problem is you think you have time."

Buddha

In June 2006, I found an old bucket list that I had written three years earlier and I realised I'd spent more time staring out of the window and going on random YouTube frenzies than I had trying to achieve my goals. I was no nearer to completing it than when I wrote it.

1. Emigrate to Australia

2. Live in an outback town

3. Swim with Great White Sharks in South Africa

4. Trek the Inca Trail, Peru

5. Visit Machu Picchu, Mexico

6. Circumnavigate the globe visiting New York, Las Vegas, Los Angeles, San Francisco

7. Write a book

A list without ACTION is just a list. You wouldn't write out your shopping list and just expect your shopping to come to you, would you? I had read every book and listened to every Tony Robbins box set he had ever sold. I knew what I had to do, I just wasn't doing it. In Tim Urban's words, the 'instant gratification monkey' was sailing the ship. Why plan

to emigrate to Australia when you can fly to Ibiza and go clubbing with your mates instead? It was getting myself to take action that was the problem. I needed to break my goals down into manageable size pieces. Once I'd done that, I gave them each a deadline and wrote down one action I could take straight away to accomplish each goal. It's all about momentum. I wrote out, "I will be in Australia by January 2008." Then I sat down at the computer and revamped my resume so it was ready to send out. Thanks to Tony, the ball was finally rolling.

Two weeks later, I saw an ad in the newspaper for Western Australia Police. As if by divine intervention, they were recruiting police officers from the UK. I sent my C.V. off straight away. Within the month, I received an invite to Australia House for a psychometric assessment and presentation from the recruitment team. The ball was rolling a little too fast.

The day before the session, I was working with Gary one of the Queen's corridor officers. I told him I was unsure about going to Australia House. I had cold feet.

"Well a' think ya would be a fool not t' go," he said in his Geordie accent.

As we were talking a lady wearing bright pink ear muffs approached the gate. Gary went over and they started chatting. I overheard her saying she was visiting from Perth, Australia.

"I'm here on a recruitment drive with Western Australia Police," she said.

"Really?" said Gary with a big grin on his face, "And what is it that you do?"

"I'm in charge of the psychometric testing," she replied.

Gary turned to me and said, "If that's not a sign a' don't know wha' is."

Who was I to argue with such a synchronistic event? I introduced 'pink ear muff lady' to my Inspector and he invited her onto the forecourt to watch the changing of the guard. This privilege usually entails an application and a four-month wait. She stood there wearing her pink ear muffs and a big grin. My Inspector gave her the obligatory glowing reference of course.

The following day she met me at Australia House minus the pink ear muffs. She introduced me to the Inspector and Sergeant in charge of recruiting and then led me to my seat in front of the other 80 candidates.

Teacher's pet...

As the test started, I looked around the room. Everyone else was frantically scribbling on their papers. It was all a bit serious. I looked at the question. They were obscure to say the least.

1. Do you ever feel like people are following you?
    a) Never
    b) Sometimes
    c) Chocolate.
    d) Only on a full moon. ✓

2. Do you ever hear voices in your head?
    a) No.
    b) Who said that?
    c) Daffodils.
    d) Only on a Wednesday ✓

The test went on for over two hours and towards the end, I was just scribbling through any letter in an attempt to get it finished. I didn't think for a moment that I had passed. Three weeks later I received a

letter congratulating me on passing the I.Q. and psychometric testing and inviting me for a formal interview at Australia House.

You are joking...

I guess I am living proof that you can cheat a psychometric test. It felt like the Universe was conspiring to get me to WA despite my attempts to sabotage it.

I arrived early for the interview and sat there nervously. The Inspector called me in to the interview room where the Sergeant and a civilian member of staff were sitting at a round table. It felt quite informal.

The civilian lady said in opening, "So, I have to ask, what's the Queen like?"

That just made me laugh, but it broke the ice and let us get on with the more pressing questions such as, "How do you think you'll cope with the climate and the wildlife?" and "Have you done your sums? Can you afford to emigrate?"

I left Australia House feeling quietly confident. Four weeks later I finally received the letter saying "Congratulations, when can you start?" I had been talking about emigrating for years and now it was all going ahead, I was absolutely petrified.

How scary...

Anyone who has ever made a massive lifestyle change such as emigrating will tell you that uprooting yourself from everything familiar and comfortable is not easy. Friends and family may also start to pull at the old heart strings. Stay true to yourself. Ask yourself if you are making the change for the right reasons. Plenty of people run away from their old lives looking for something better only to find when they get there, they still have all the same problems they had before.

The Passenger

An empty bridge, a Captain-less ship,
Its course already set,
The dark and sea worn vessel,
Sails out across the harbour's edge.

One soul on board with one purpose,
Looks out through the velvety night.
Endlessly searching the horizon,
For that part of itself that took flight.

The long, distant journey now over,
The Passenger prepares to alight.
A smoky silhouette on the gangway,
A familiar face cloaked in the moonlight.

Her eyes find yours and she smiles,
You stand frozen in disbelief.
She has sailed for thousands of miles,
And a further thousand if need be.

There is no place left to run,
Nowhere to hide her pursue.
She will find you wherever you go,
The one you are running from, is You.

Change your city, your country, your home,
You're still the same person inside.
It matters not how far you roam,
If it is from yourself, you are trying to hide...

I thought long and hard about why I wanted to leave the UK. Maybe part of me was running away, but I was also running toward something better. Of course I wanted the beach, the weather and the lifestyle, but more importantly, I felt like I had stopped growing. I desperately needed change. I was craving variety, a challenge. A new start. But did I want it enough? After all, London had been home for years. I had my own place, I had a well-paid, comfortable job that I knew like the back of my hand. I was at a cross road. What if things didn't work out? What if I hated it? What if the Met wouldn't take me back?

I read an article once about why some people succeed in life and some don't. It said, imagine we are all standing at the door to a corridor stretching out into the darkness. Those that were successful were those that were able to lean into their fears, risking uncertainty and launch themselves down the corridor without any guarantees of success. Once there, other doors (opportunities) opened up that they wouldn't have seen had they not taken that leap. Most people let their fears stop them taking action. They wait until they have guarantees or assurances, or they wait for the time to be just right, but as James Clear said, "Successful people start before they're ready."

I realised that the time was never going to be just right. I typed out my resignation letter and walked over to our H.R. office. I stood there outside the office holding this piece of paper. It was just a piece of paper but it signified the end of a twelve-year Met Police career. I took a deep breath, walked into the office and handed it in to our senior admin officer. There was no fanfare, she just confirmed that my last day was the 16th December 2007. That was it.

I was finally in the hallway of crippling uncertainty. I felt like a tight rope walker without a net. The world suddenly seemed very large and scary.

"Leap and the net will appear…"

John Burroughs

Clearing out my flat felt very liberating. I had no idea how much material things actually weighed you down until I was free of them. I left the UK in January 2008, with just a rucksack on my back and a phone number of a friend in Perth.

When I finally touched down in Australia the Immigration officer stamped my passport, smiled and said, "Welcome home Ms. Williams."

I finally made it. I was in Australia. I was home.

I have been in Australia for the past eight years, four years of which I spent in Kalgoorlie, an outback gold mining town. These past few years have been some of the happiest of my life. I have made some close friends, travelled to some amazing places and worked in some fascinating towns and communities. I live near the beach and my drive into work takes me up the West Coast Highway overlooking the Indian Ocean, with its beautiful blue skies and palm trees. It beats the Victoria Line any day. I am extremely grateful to be here and the more grateful I am, the happier I feel. Funny that.

Lisa also applied for an Australian visa and with her Master's degree in Social Work, they practically threw the visa at her. I feel blessed that she is now living down the road with her family and I can pop over for Sunday dinner and hang out with my nephew Dylan. It's the small things.

With this final chapter now written, I have completed everything on my first list. I am already working my way through the second, which includes another book about my Australian adventures. I want to experience as much of life as possible, so I will be able to look back without regret.

A blackboard was put up in New York for a day asking people to write down their biggest regret. One word came up over and over again; Not. Not taking chances. Not following my dreams. Not saying I love you. Not finishing my degree. Not speaking my mind. Not starting my own business. People like to stay in their barren little comfort zones. Nothing grows there. All growth begins at the end of our comfort zone.

If you want to go back to college and do a degree, send off for the application. If you want to run your own business, speak to your bank about a loan. If you want to write a book, just start writing. Write a list and take some action towards it **today**. Time is the most precious gift we have been given, yet we gamble with it every day, not knowing when our chips are going to get cashed in. If I have one regret, it is that I didn't take action much sooner. I just kept waiting for the right time. But the truth is, there is no right time. There is only **now**.

"The best time to plant a tree was 20 years ago. The second best time is now."

Chinese Proverb

- Your greatest gift may be hiding behind your greatest fear. Take risks.

- Happiness is the result of gratitude. Appreciate the small things.

- Write down your goals and put dates on them. Take ONE action toward that goal straight away.

- There are opportunities waiting in the corridor. Take a leap of faith.

Author Profile

Cat Williams

Author, Police Officer and Philanthropist

Cat is an author, police officer and philanthropist who lives a life of service.

Voted most likely to end up in prison by her former school teacher, she began her career in the British Army. Awarded Top Recruit in basic training and Best Recruit of the Year in her regiment, Cat went on to become the first female to be awarded First Place on a Royal Engineers Junior NCO cadre.

Upon leaving the Army, she joined the London Metropolitan Police. While there, she spent six years serving in the Royalty Protection Squad at Buckingham Palace. She then migrated to Western Australia and spent four years working as a police officer in Kalgoorlie an outback gold mining town.

Her mother died of breast cancer when she was six. After her younger sister's breast cancer diagnosis in 2014, Cat was inspired to take part in charity events to benefit breast cancer support and research. She has completed a parachute jump for Macmillan Cancer Support, shaved her head for the World's Greatest Shave charity event, took part in the 200km Ride to Conquer Cancer and will donate 20% of the profits from her book sales to the Harry Perkins Institute for cancer research.

Additionally, she has cycled from London to Paris for Success for Kids children's charity and hiked the Inca trail in Peru for the Great Ormond Street Children's hospital, London.

Cat has lived, travelled, and worked throughout the United Kingdom, Portugal, Borneo, Spain, France, Germany, Cyprus, Singapore, The Netherlands, South Africa, Egypt, Canada, the United States, Mexico, Thailand, Hong Kong, Indonesia, Australia and New Zealand.

Cat Williams is the author of "From Prison to Palace" and lives in Perth, Australia. She is also a Certified Robbins-Madanes Strategic Intervention coach, specialising in relationship issues.